Road

A play

Jim Cartwright

Samuel French - London
New York - Toronto - Hollywood

ROAD

First performed at the Royal Court Theatre Upstairs,
London, on 22nd March, 1986, with the following cast.
Then transferring to the Royal Court's main auditorium
on 9th June 1986.

Scullery	Edward Tudor-Pole
Carol's Mother	Susan Brown
Carol	Mossie Smith
Louise	Lesley Sharp
Brink	Neil Dudgeon
Eddie's Dad	Colin McCormack
Eddie	William Armstrong
Molly	Susan Brown
Professor	Colin McCormack
Skin	William Armstrong
Helen	Susan Brown
Jerry	Colin McCormack
Joey	Neil Dudgeon
Clare	Lesley Sharp

Other parts

Dor	Mossie Smith	**Lane**	Lesley Sharp
Marion	Susan Brown	**Brian**	Colin McCormack
Clint	William Armstrong		
		Chantal	Mossie Smith
Linda	Lesley Sharp		
Bisto	William Armstrong	**Mr Bald** **Mrs Bald**	Neil Dudgeon
Tom Stanley	Neil Dudgeon	**Chance Peterson**	Colin McCormack
Blowpipe	William Armstrong	**Barry**	William Armstrong
Chipshop Girl	Gail Pallin	**Electric Clutch**	Mossie Smith, Lesley Sharp and Susan Brown

The play directed by **Simon Curtis**
Produced by **Max Stafford-Clark**
Designed by **Paul Brown**

Road returned to the Royal Court's main auditorium in January 1987 with the following cast of characters:

Scullery	Ian Dury
Louise	Jane Horrocks
Brother	Ewan Stewart
Brenda	Susan Brown
Carol	Mossie Smith
Brink	Ewan Stewart
Eddie	Iain Glen
Eddie's Dad	Alan David
Molly	Susan Brown
Professor	Alan David
Chantal	Mossie Smith
Skin	Iain Glen
Jerry	Alan David
Clare	Jane Horrocks
Joey	Ewan Stewart
Helen	Susan Brown
Valerie	Jane Horrocks

All other parts played by members of the company

The play directed by **Simon Curtis**
Designed by **Paul Brown**

CHARACTERS

Scullery
Brenda, Carol's mother
Barry
Louise, a young girl
Louise's Brother
Carol, a young girl
Brink, a young man
Eddie's Dad
Eddie, a young lad
Dor ⎫
Lane ⎭ tarted-up women
Skin-Lad
Molly, an old woman
The Professor
Chantal, a young girl of about 16
Bald
Mrs Bald
Jerry, a middle-aged man
Blowpipe
Clare, a young girl of about 16
Joey, a young lad of about 17
Bisto, a DJ
Tom Stanley, pub compère
Electric Clutch, 3 dancers
Manfred, chip shop owner
Scotch Girl, his assistant
Curt, a young lad
Helen, a middle-aged woman
Soldier
Valerie, a woman in her mid-30s
Marion, a drunk woman
Linda, a girl of about 12

The action of the play takes place in a road in a small Lancashire town

Time—tonight

PRODUCTION NOTE

There was a pre-show (described on page 1) to the Royal Court production, if this is not used the show begins with Scullery's speech on page 3.

Three episodes in the script may be shortened, if preferred, and these are given in a section at the end of the main text.

ACT I

PRE-SHOW

In the street in front of the theatre, Chantal (a young girl from Road, about sixteen but simple-minded) is hanging around or going up and down on a little child's shove scooter. After a while she is joined by Linda, another girl from Road, about twelve. She is in her night-dress, and has sneaked out to play before going to bed. They sit on the theatre steps and play chalk games, sometimes obscene. As the time for the performance approaches, the House Manager of the theatre should come out and tell them to clear off

As this is occurring outside, inside the theatre bar has been converted into the Millstone Pub, *a typical old Lancashire pub, with a dartboard, a little tiny stage in the corner, with mike and glitter ribbons behind, for the pub entertainers to perform on, posters advertising the "Pub Disco Room" with "Bisto and his Beatoven Disco", pub lunches, trips, photographs advertising tonights's turns: "Chance Peterson, singer", "Tom Stanley, your compère", "The Electric Clutch, erotic dancers", etc. Barry is in the pub playing darts. The following scene was used as a basis for the bar improvisation. It should be noted that this is a scene only to be passed through or by, and not the start of the play and should be very low-key, slow, natural and lengthy, almost unnoticeable*

Barry is in the pub playing darts

Brenda comes in and goes to the bar

Brenda Hey mate. Can I have a drink on t'slate, eh. Summat on t'slate. I'm skint you see, until me daughter gi's me some later. She comes in here, Carol, you know her. Gi'us one an she'll pay you later. Eh. Eh. Go on lovey, gi'us a bottle. Oh sod off then. Stuck up flea. (*She turns round and sees Barry*) Barry! Baz! Playin' darts then Baza.

He ignores her

What time is it, Bar?
Barry Dunno.
Brenda What ha'you doing in so early, Bar?

He ignores her

Eh what's so early for?
Barry I'm waitin' for John to play pool.
Brenda Ay, lend us a cig.

He plays on

A cig, Bar.

He plays on

Lend us a cig.

Barry gives her one. He plays on

Got a light, Bar.

He plays

Got a light, Barry?

He throws his lighter at her, plays on. She picks it up, lights up, pockets the lighter. She watches the game, watches the game

Want a pound on one?

He ignores her. She watches

Wan' a pound on one?

He ignores, she watches

Wan' a pound on one?
Barry BLOODY HELL!
Brenda Do you though, Bar?
Barry EH!
Brenda Want a pound on one. I've no drink money, does see Bar? But it might be me lucky day eh, might it, Bar.
Barry Alreet then. (*He starts walking to the bar*)
Brenda Reet. God I've gone thirsty I always do when I'm coming up to play.
Barry (*to the Barman*) 'Nother set o' darts, cock.

The Barman passes them over the bar to Barry. Brenda is disappointed—she thought he was going for drinks

Here. (*He shoves them in her hand*)

They go to the board and play the first set

Brenda You chalk up Bar, I can't do take-aways.

As he goes up to the blackboard, she takes a quick sip of his drink. They play another set. She's waiting for him to go to the board again. But this time he downs his in one then goes to the board to chalk up

Do you want another then, Barry? (*To the Barman*) He might want another here in a sec, love.

Barry is returning

Do you, Bar?
Barry What?

Brenda Want another ale.

Barry Shut up an' play if you're playing.

Brenda I'll have to whether I want to or not, won't a. I need that pound more than me next breath Baz, I'll tell you that. I mean remember you're playing a girl.

He's gone. He is over at the bar queuing for a drink. She sneakily runs up and shoves the darts in the board, then runs back to the spot

Brenda One hundred and eighty! One hundred and eighty! Look at that, Barry, look.

Barry goes to the board takes the darts out

Barry Game's over.

Brenda Eh?

Barry Game's over Brenda.

Brenda Well what about fifty p for a good try.

Barry (*carrying on playing on his own*) Go.

Brenda runs in front of the dartboard

Move Brenda or I'll throw this right in the cow's eye.

Brenda (*beaten; under her breath*) Fuck you.

She goes

Meanwhile, in the auditorium Scullery is there on stage or on the floor to greet the audience as they come in. On stage Eddie's Dad is in his house, sitting on an armchair, fixing a Hoover across his knee, the TV on. In another house, Louise's Brother is sitting on a chair fixing an oily engine. Brenda enters her house and sits in an armchair smoking, tense. When all the audience are in and settled, Act I begins

"Somewhere Over the Rainbow" by Judy Garland is playing. The record ends

Blackness

A match is struck. It is held underneath a broken road sign. The name part has been ripped off, leaving a sharp, twisted, jagged edge, only the word "Road" is left. The sign is very old and has been this way a long time

Scullery It's been broken.

The flame moves across to illuminate Scullery's face. He holds the match there until it goes out; at the same time a spotlight creeps up on his face

Wid' your night yous chose to come and see us. Wid' our night as usual we's all gettin' ready and turning out for a drink. THIS IS OUR ROAD! But tonight it's your road an' all! Don't feel awkward wi' us, make yourselves at home. You'll meet "all-sorts" down here, I'm telling you love. An' owt can happen tonight. He might get a bird. She might ha' a fight, she might. Let's shove off down t'Road and find out! We'll go down house by house. Hold tight! Here we go! Come on! (*He beckons the audience around*) Watch the kerb missis! Road's coming round us! (*He starts laughing, laughing uproariously*)

Black-out, then the Lights come up on a living-room. There is a mirror up at the back. A man (Louise's Brother) in a vest, and old trousers and socks, is sitting in a chair, leaning over and working on an oily (car, bike, or machine) engine, on spread-out newspapers

A young girl, Louise, bursts in, dressed for going out, frantically brushing her hair

Louise Late, late again, late. Can I get to mirror?
Brother Shut it.

She has to try and do it from where she is

Louise Where's Mum and Dad?
Brother (*mouthing*) Shagging.
Louise Is they!

He looks at her in disbelief, shakes his head, carries on

I wish to God you wun't joke me like that. I could just imagine 'em there then, on that dirty bed of vests.

He just ignores her, carries on

You not going out?

He stares at her. She jumps in fear. She carries on brushing. She looks round

Where's dog?
Brother Out back.
Louise Have you fed him today?
Brother (*not looking up*) Fuck facey, fuck facey. Fuck facey. Fuck facey. Fuck off. Fuck off.
Louise Why do you never go out, you?
Brother Can't afford it. Why do you never stay in?
Louise I can't stand it.

Brother throws the engine at her. She jumps back, screams

You think you're scary. But you're just a big lump of it.

Brother turns the chair over. His next line though not said in an overtly sexual way, carries sexual threat

Brother Let's dance.
Louise (*scared*) You can't dance with your brother.
Brother I know. Everything's not allowed in life. (*He takes two quid out, gives it to her*) Here.
Louise Where's that from?
Brother (*indicating the engine*) I'm doing a job for Eric.
Louise (*holding the money*) You go an' get a pint on it.
Brother No, I've got a quarter-bottle under me pillow.
Louise You're not going back to bed is you, you're there all day and night.

Brother Do you want a punch?

Louise No.

Brother I wish you did. I'd love to see summat' go down. (*He looks at his oily hands*) I'm going for a bath.

Louise Don't put the immersion on, me mum 'ull kill you.

He puts his hands on her face. Then draws them down her cheeks, smudging make-up and leaving black

Oh no! I'm goin' be really late now. I'm going have go up and do it again. I'm goin' be late late now. You pigging bastard.

She goes up

He looks out after her, starts clapping, clapping his hands for a long time. He suddenly stops

Brother (*blankly to the audience*) Fucking long life innit.

Black-out. The Lights come up on another living-room. An old beaten red armchair, an ironing-board up at the back. Brenda, a thin wizened scruffy woman sits in the chair facing the audience, smoking. At the back, Carol in bra and knickers is ironing her dress

Brenda (*who speaks in a low, quiet, one-tone voice*) Where you goin'?

Carol Out.

Brenda Where you goin'?

Carol Out.

Brenda Where you goin'?

Carol The pub.

Brenda Tha's better. What time you be back?

Carol Whenever.

Brenda What time you be back?

Carol Whenever.

Brenda What time?

Carol Eleven, twelve-ish.

Brenda Tha's better. Are you still seeing that lad?

Carol I'm not answering any more questions.

Brenda There you are then. Don't bring anyone back here the night.

Carol As though I would.

Brenda You would. You would. I'm sick of the sound of it down here.

Carol What do you mean?

Brenda You know.

Carol Look leave me alone, I'm ironing this.

Brenda Well speak then.

Carol Look why should I eh? You're nothing to me.

Brenda I'm Mother.

Carol You're my mother so what?

Brenda I'm your mother and I brung you from ... (*She indicates with her hand*) ... that to that!

Carol Ay ay well I'm leaving soon. So thanks an' all that, but there you are.

Brenda Ay here I am and there you are so let's have something.
Carol What?
Brenda Respect and money.
Carol I'll give you your money Monday morning and your respects down
  the bog.
Brenda Pissing young git.

*There is the sound of someone shouting and laughing. They both get up and
lean out front*

Carol }
Brenda } *(together)* SHUT IT!!

They look at each other and laugh. They go back to ironing and sitting

Brenda Have you had 'owt eat.
Carol I've had a warmed-up pastie from dinner.
Brenda Well get summat else.
Carol What else? There's rock all in, but shrunk carrots, Sugar Puffs, and
  some spit or summat in a saucer.
Brenda Don't exaggerate.
Carol Uh.
Brenda Anyway get summat down you before you go out.
Carol You get summat down you.
Brenda You get summat down you.
Carol You get summat down you.
Brenda You get summat down you.
Carol You get summat down you.
Brenda You get summat down you.
Carol You get summat down you. You're the one whose goin' to be pissed
  up and lying in it.
Brenda Shove it you little tart.
Carol You shove it.

Carol turns the dress over, spits on the iron, carries on

Brenda So you're goin' down the boozer are you?
Carol Yeah. Are you?
Brenda I might go down if somebody coughs up.
Carol Are you still going with that ragman?
Brenda No.
Carol Why not?
Brenda He snotted off din't he. He owes me an' all.
Carol Eh?
Brenda Yeah like you all do, every one of yous. I s'pose you're skint an' all.
Carol Well I've got some but I need it for tonight.
Brenda Well give it me.
Carol No.
Brenda Yes.
Carol No.
Brenda Yes.

Carol No.

Brenda Yes.

Carol No, you mouldy old slag.

Brenda Yes, you young pig.

Carol Cow!

Brenda Sick!

Carol Oh God, you're crude. How could I have let you bring me up. Fling me up more like, I was flung through the years.

Brenda Listen her romanticizing. You've done all right out of my bones you lot.

Carol You're nothing but bones anyway. Why don't you eat?

Brenda Because I don't. Because I don't. I do any way. I get enough.

Carol You'd rather swill ale. Wun't you? Look at you. Your skin's like ham. There's veins showing all over you. You're hung in your old clothes. You never wash, you never change. You never ... never ... (*She can't bring herself to say it*) I'm like I am because of you and you're like you are because of who knows what rot. (*She puts her dress on. It is very short*) Is it short enough for you?

Brenda Ask men.

A loud knocking on the door

Carol Come in Louise!

Carol puts her coat on
   Louise comes in, she looks upset

Louise (*to both*) Hello.

Brenda (*uninterested*) Hiyah.

Carol (*to Louise*) What's up with you?

Louise Me shoulder pad's slipped.

Carol Pissing hell Louise, there's always summat wi' you.

They set off

Brenda Are you giving me some?

Carol I can let you have a pound.

Brenda Oh generous. Generous. Generosity. Generosity. Generous.

Carol throws change all over the floor, then walks out with Louise
Brenda scurries and scrambles on the floor for money. She stops on all fours, looks to the audience

Brenda Fucking long life innit.

The Lights come up on the road
   Scullery enters, with a bottle

Scullery All right? (*He nods to someone in the audience, offers a drink to another*) Do you want one, luv? (*He drinks*) This is my domain. I'm in and out everywhere here, all about. There's everything you needs, two pubs at the top, chippy round the side, places to hide. This road and me. (*He pours some rum on the Road*) Have one. What a fuckin' place though!

Carol and Louise pass

Carol *The Millstone. The Swan. The Blue Boar. The New Zealand Chief. Ikey's. Wheatsheaf. Gypsy's Tent.*
Louise *White Horse. Market. Ancient Shepherd. Smokey's. The Millstone.*
Scullery My darlings.

They run off squealing and laughing

Carol (*off*) Fuck off, Scullery!
Scullery Come and taste me!
Carol (*shouting off*) No way, your fly's full of fleas!
Scullery Please yourself, chickens. You can't escape! (*He blows a kiss after them, winks then drinks*) Let me help you get your bearings. There's the town, there's this Road, then there's the slag heap. This is the last stop. All of life is chucked here. You've seen nowt yet. There's auld Molly at number seven, there's the Professor in the end house there, there's Skin-Lad at number fourteen, he's a fucking nutter. There's all-sorts. Nature is above us, there's moon, there's stars, there's the Plough, there's the fucking what's-'is-name. Moon's coming up full, I feel full, I feel full and cocked and I'll tell you what, stick wi' me tonight, stick wi' Scullery.

The sound of someone whistling is heard. A young man, Brink, comes across the stage, whistling, in a suit. Handsome, slow-walking

Hiyah lad.
Brink (*keeps walking*) All right, Scullery.
Scullery Is it Brink?
Brink Ay.
Scullery Have you got a ciggy, lad?
Brink Ay. (*He goes over to him, gives him one*)
Scullery Ay. Where you off?
Brink Eddie's. (*He lights the cigarette for him*)
Scullery Eddie's eh?

Brink starts to walk away

See you.
Brink See you.

Brink exits

Scullery Eddie's eh. Let's have a see.

Black-out

The Lights come up on a room. There is a television up back facing the audience and an old armchair facing the television. Eddie's Dad is in the chair, his back to the audience, fixing a Hoover. The TV is up full rocketing blast. Front stage, a young lad, Eddie, topless, is combing his wet hair back and back to shape it, looking in a mirror on the wall*. Knock knock at the door

He goes out to answer it and comes in with Brink

*See production note p. 57

Brink waves at Eddie's Dad. He doesn't look up. Brink sits at the table near Eddie. He lights up another cigarette. Eddie carries on. He takes a shirt off the back of the chair and puts it on. He takes it off, angry. He gets an anti-perspirant off the chair, sprays under his arms, still looking in the mirror. Some spray goes over near Brink. Brink leans right back hands up. Eddie turns and sprays his Dad's head. Eddie puts his shirt on again. He gets his tie off the back of the chair and puts it on, looking in the mirror. Angry again, he takes the tie off. He ties it again

Brink Where we goin'?
Eddie (*not looking round, repeating what he thought he heard*) What? Where we goin'?
Brink (*can't hear*) Eh?
Eddie (*exasperated*) Fucking hell. (*He reaches for his aftershave; puts it on*)

A loud knocking on the wall. Eddie grabs a pan and starts knocking back. The knocking stops. Eddie does one more knock, then throws the pan down. He puts his jacket on

Come on then.
Brink (*doesn't hear*) Eh?

Eddie, exasperated, just heads for the door. Brink stubs his fag out and follows. Eddie holds the door open. Brink goes out. Eddie looks at the man in the chair, then goes out, slamming the door

Eddie's Dad gets up, turns the TV off, plugs the Hoover in and vacuums in detail the exact spot where Eddie was standing

Black-out

The Lights find Scullery. He is sitting high above, bottle in hand. (He's got up there by ladder, rubble, or drain pipe?)

Scullery Arghhh that lovely smell of the night, my favourite. I sniff it into me blood, sniff (*he does*) sniff (*he does*). Get's me high as a kite.

Brink and Eddie pass

All right lads, where you off?
Eddie Pub after pub.
Scullery Well save some birds for me!
Brink Nay Scullery the early worm snatches the birds.

They exit

Scullery Eeee I feel randy me now, you know. It's like on the ships when you get it on you you's nowhere to turn.

He sees Dor and Lane enter—two tarted-up women

Here you're OK though down the Road, down the alley, the alley alley oh.

Lane is singing "The Lady is a Tramp"

Scullery wolf-whistles from above. They look up

Dor }
Lane } *(together)* SCULLERY!
Scullery Doreen. Lane. Where you off?
Lane Every pub in sight.

Lane and Dor laugh

Dor What's that?
Scullery Rum.
Dor Give us some.
Scullery Come up here then.
Dor No way.

Lane looks up, weighing the distance, grabs Dor's mouth, opens it and walks her forward

Lane Here pour it in, Scullery.

Scullery leans over, aiming the bottle

Up a bit, stop. Left a bit. Stop. Down a bit, stop. Pour.

He does. It goes all over her face. Lane and Scullery have a good laugh

Scullery Come up!
Lane I'm going up, me. (*She does*)
Dor Hang on then.

They set off up

(*Pulling her skirt in, to the audience*) Don't look.

Lane gets up first, sits beside Scullery

Scullery What a view!
Dor Eh! Oh I thought you meant up me gusset. (*She clambers down beside them*)
Scullery No, the ROAD.
Lane To me it's like ... What's that thing you have in t' Gents?
Dor Trough.
Lane Thanks Doreen. It's like a long pissie trough to me.
Scullery (*lifting his coat sides for them*) Anyway get stuck in girls wherever you want.
Dor No way, I've just scrubbed me nails.
Lane (*taking the bottle, reading*) Navy rum. You were at sea once weren't you, Scullery?
Scullery Ay Ay the big ships.
Lane I thought you had the twang of the sea.
Dor Shiver me timbers.
Lane Come on let's hoist the riggin'.

She jumps on him, they kiss

Skin-Lad comes running on

Dor Oooh eh look here!

They come up from the kiss

Skin-Lad passes

Dor ⎫
Lane ⎭ (*together*) Whooooooooooooooooooooooo.

Scullery SKIN-LAD!

Scullery ⎫
Dor   ⎬ (*together*) He's a fucking nutter!
Lane ⎭

They all laugh. Scullery grabs Lane again for more. They kiss on. Dor decides to get down and go

Dor See you in *Mill Stone* later, Lane.
Lane (*still snogging, muffled*) See you, Dor.
Dor (*mumbling as she goes*) Snog anything she will. Captain fucking Pugwash.

Dor exits

Scullery and Lane come up for air

Lane Where'd you get that devil kiss?
Scullery The tropics.
Lane Ooooooooh take me round world, snog by snog. Start wi' France.

They kiss. Black-out

Silence. Then some sounds of Road. The sound of a window opening, a voice at breaking point: "Fucking fuck"—the window closes. Silence. A dog starts barking. It stops. From somewhere else, the sound of someone crying. It stops. Silence. The Lights come up on a little room: sink, table and chair, cooker. An old woman in overcoat and slippers is there. She is emptying a bucket down the sink. She goes and sits at the table

Molly Dreamy dreamy dreamy dream tu ti tum tum tum tum tum.

On the table is a box full of old make-up. She starts putting lipstick on her frail lips, looking in a little mirror

Bit o' red. (*She looks in the mirror*) Bit more o' red. (*She gets up, goes and fills the kettle*) I'll have some tea in between (*She starts filling the kettle. She looks out dreaming. The kettle overflows. She stops*) Oh oh. Imagine that. (*She pours the water away, and puts the kettle on the cooker*) Dreamy dreamy dream dreamy. (*She lights the gas*) Dreamy dolly day dream. Where was we. (*She looks round, lost. She goes back and puts a teabag in a cup. She stands waiting for the kettle to boil. She sings*) Here's me in me likkle house, havin' some tea in between, in between dolling up for a drink, a drink, a drink. I'm standing by me sink. Here's likkle me.

The kettle boils. She puts her hand in her coat cuff and pulls the kettle off. She pours it into the cup. She looks round

No milk you silly dilk, no sugar you daft likkle bugger. (*She goes back to the table with the teacup. She looks back, sees something below the sink. She sings*) There's milk you silly dilk, you looks round, some is found. Do a likkle twinkle dance. (*She does a little shuffling dance step as she goes over to it. She picks up the cat's saucer and pours a drop in her cup. She puts the saucer down and sits. She starts again on her make-up. She takes an eyebrow pencil out of the box, and looks in the mirror*) Old eyebrows (*She starts drawing over her eyebrows*) Good thing you're a good drawer. You can get round the curves wid' your fancy hands. (*She stops, looks up*) He could, that bust-squeezer. He pushed them from the top down this-away. He see'd me through half the war that man. Stroking, silent, never speaking. Did he die? (*She reaches out*) I can't see his face. (*She hits her temple*) I need a new aerial. (*She takes a sip of her tea*) Dreamy one, likkle me, doll dream. (*She carries on. She comes to powder*) Powder up. (*She puts powder on a puff*) Alli-up (*She puts it on her face, it all scatters. She coughs*) Puts me in mind of Kenny, Kenny Howcroft the homo. With his big white handbag. A sweet 'un. We used to drink gin off each other's fingers down the bar. (*She looks up*) Naughty nincompoops. (*She sips her tea, crinkles her nose*) I used to crinkle my nose like this. (*She crinkles her nose. She starts on her hair, gets a brush and combs a strand up*) Go up hair, up up. Come on now. Go as I say. Curly curly wurly crackle. My mother used to do it hundred times before bed. Long, white it was. (*Looking out, she goes down with her hand as though touching it. She puts her hand lightly at her throat, looking out for a long time. Pause. Still looking. Silence. Still looking. She takes her teacup, sips*) Tea's coldish (*She shivers*) There's a chill in the air. (*She looks out again. Pause*) I'll git meself ready and turn out. (*She picks up the little mirror and carries on*)

Black-out

The Lights come up on the Road

Professor appears (among the audience or on stage), glasses crooked and falling off, scruffy old clothes. He carries a long cardboard box under his arm full of papers, and an old, little, battered portable cassette tape recorder

Professor (*to someone in the audience*) I'm the Professor me. I'm not really a professor, I'm just a nosy bastard who wants to try everything. When I got made redundant I decided to do an anthropological study of "Road" and go down in history. So I moved in the end house here. But all I did was go down. I lost me wife, me family, half me stomach, everything. Now all I got left is this tape, and this box full of all me records, all I could write really. Long agos I gived up the idea of making a book, and instead, now I just give 'em out to people for the price of a pint or chips. (*He plucks out a piece of paper from the box, clears his throat, then reads the title*) "Social Life in Road: Wood Street Drinking Club. An episode that occured in winter of Our Lord nineteen eighty-two. I went in. A woman was crapping behind the piano. Two men were fighting over a pie. A row of old prostitutes were sitting there, still made up as in war years. Price tags on the sole of their shoes which they kick up at you as you walk by. I chose the three pounds thirty-two one and bent her over the billiard table in the back room. Nobody saw. I could tell she didn't like it so I spoke to her afterwards. She said she had to do it to keep her four kids decent. I told her three pounds thirty-two wasn't much, she said she wasn't much and come to that neither was I. That's where we left it." See how easy you can slip when you's a scientist in the slums.

Lane has entered earlier and has been listening from a distance

Lane Prof!

Professor (*seeing her*) Lane love.

They embrace

Lane I'll give you one on Wood Street.

He gets the tape recorder out, turns it on, holds the mike out

Piano, you got splinters if you put your hand on it. Walls, spit yellow. Tables, soaked in beer, The club. The people, There was Slack-mouth, Wriggle.

Professor Donny.

Lane Mrs Walmsley.

Professor P. H. Pye.

Lane Oh ay. Face like a throat.

Professor Lake Walter.

Lane What a drinker.

Professor Nelly.

Lane Oh ay Nelly. Sixty-eight years old and still on the game. But she had that senile habit of wantin' sex on the cobbles. Well, when a man walked in wi' no knees you knew he'd been up Nelly.

Professor (*into the mike*) Memories of Wood Street.

Lane It were a bad bastard day when they closed it. My friend slashed on the town hall steps in protest. But it were done with. Put us all in t'doldrums.

Professor You mention dole there. I'll give you one from my dole records. (*He takes a piece of paper out, clears his throat, reads*) "Study of Unemployment in Road. Bill, forty-two: 'You wake up, you look out from under. There's nowhere to go. Your wife's up, she can't sleep, she's counting and pinching pennies all night. My kids are in t'next room in old jumble-sale pyjamas. What the fucking hell's happening to me?' Larry, twenty-eight: 'You get depressed. It's like black water droppin'. You feel it in the chest.' "

Lane You morbid bastard. Life's a spree, Prof. Me and Dor we get our mouth round life and have a chew, sometimes there's nowt, sometimes it's sloppy, but we keep on snoggin' through. (*She slaps his cheeks*) See you later, Prof.

Lane exits

Chantal walks on singing a little child's song. She comes across Scullery

The Professor watches

Chantal Scullery, got a light?

Scullery What's it worth?

Chantal holds two fags up, one for him. He takes a cig, then lights hers

Chantal (*looking at the lighter*) Where'd you get that?

Scullery Spoils of war, my dear hearty.

Chantal Ummmmmmmmmmmmmmmmmmmmmmmmm.

She sets off. Suddenly the cardboard box goes skidding across the stage, and stops in front of her. She stops, looks at it. The Professor speedily wobbles over, stooping, almost sitting on the box

Professor Excuse me, my dear, is there any way well . . .?

She smiles, walks off singing the little child's song. He follows, dragging his cardboard box by its loose string

Scullery draws on his fag. The sound of a window opening, and of the "Dynasty" theme tune on TV inside. Something hits the ground near Scullery, the window closes, Scullery picks it up, it's a piece of paper; he unfolds it

Scullery (*reading*) "Dear Scullery, You remind me of a famous star but I can't think of his name. Also you are sex mad. You can come up after if you want. When he's gone out. Also have a wash. Love, Girly. PS. This paper is well-snogged." (*He looks out to the audience. He screws up the piece of paper and drops it down his pants*)

Black-out

The Lights come up on a young man sitting on a wooden chair. A bare light bulb is dangling. He is chanting the sacred sound "Om"

Skin-Lad Ommmmmmmmmmmmmmmmmmmmmmmmmmm. He opens his eyes. He sees you. He wants to tell you the story. He feels the need to drift back on the tide of his memory, back, back, back. And I'm the lonely skinhead again. Jogging away, everyday, to be the best, to be the best. And the press-ups. And the sit-ups. And the one-two-three, one-two-three, one-two-three, one-two-three. And you've gotta be fit to fight, and I do every Saturday night, with my friends at weekends, fight. Do you know about fighting? No. I'll tell you in my story. And I want to be the best skinhead and I want to give everything, every single thing, to the experience of the tingle. I'll tell you about the tingle later. And you've gotta be fit to fight, and practise tactics every night. (*He practises*) Do you? I do. (*He practises*) Do you work in the ashfelt factory? I did. (*He practises then stops*) I'll explain. (*He indicates an imaginary opponent or a real one brought from the audience*) My opponent! Anyone you like. City fan, the cunt that shagged Ricky's bird, Ted the foreman, you choose. Targets!

(*Indicating the relevant parts on his opponent*) Face, neck, beerbag, dick, shin, top of the foot. Top of the foot. Today I want the neck, this vein here. I don't want to fuck Christine Dawson, I don't want my mother's love, I don't want to work at the engineering firm, I want the neck, this vein here. (*He practises*) Tactics, new techniques. What does he think? What do you think? (*He strikes*) The neck and that's that. He thought, you thought, the neck and that is that. Now I've told you about the three things you need to get to the experience of the tingle. One fitness, told you. Two, tactics, told you. Three, new techniques, I told you. Now I'll tell you about the tingle. (*He comes off-stage and into the audience*) Well it's ... you can't say it can you ... it'll come when you're fighting. Sometime in the middle, sometime in the beginning, sometime end, but it won't stay ... it's like you are there, you are fighting, but "you" are not there ... (*Pause*) You don't understand. (*Pause*) Anyway, once you've had it, you need it, and I thought that's all there was until that night, right, should I tell you about that night? No. I'll show you. (*He leaps back onstage*) I came out the disco, last man to leave, all my lads had gone. I'd been talking to Mickey Isherwood the bouncer. "See you Jim." "Ay, see you Ishey." Then I saw them. Skins. Bolton boot boys. Skinheads. Some sitting on the wall. Some standing. I moved off to the right. "Eh, cunty." "Eh, git head." "Come 'ere." I looked at the moon. I heard the crack of denim, the scuffle down the wall, the pad and fall of the Dr Martens, pad, pad, pad. I closed my eyes. Pad, pad. As they moved in, pad, pad, I moved out. Pad, pad. I felt their breath ... (*A loud cry*) KIYAA ... lifted one man by the chin ... can you imagine it? Magnificent ... they were scattering. Caught one man between thigh and calf, took him round to the ground, fingers up the nose, dragged a pace, nutted, lifted my fingers to pierce out his eyes, when to my surprise I saw a figure watching, like a ghost, all pale in the night. Seemed like I'd known him all my life. He was laughing at me. Mocking my whole fucking life. I sprang, when I arrived he'd gone. Too quick for me. No, I saw him disappear down a blind alley. I had him now. I had him now! He was facing the wall in a sort of peeing position. I moved in to strike, my fist was like a golden orb in the wet night, I said it was night, I struck deep and dangerous and beautiful with a twist of the fist on the out. But he was only smiling, and he opened his eyes to me like two diamonds in the night. I said it was night, and said, over to you Buddha. (*Pause*) So now I just read the dharma. And when men at work pass the pornography, I pass it on and continue with the dharma. And when my mother makes egg and bacon and chips for me I push it away towards the salt cellar and read of the dharma. And when the man on the bus push I continue with the dharma. Ommmmmmmmm

Black-out

The Road

Scullery looks up to one of the windows above him. It has sacking hanging and looks deserted

Scullery See this derelict house here? (*He takes a pillow-case out of his*

pocket and starts unfolding it) I've been meaning to give it a ransacking, see if there's any coppers to be made. You never know. (*He clambers up to the window from below. As he gets in there*)

Brenda comes on

Brenda Scullery.
Scullery Brenda. Where's that juicy daughter of yours?
Brenda Don't mention muck to me. Eh, Scullery do you remember the alley wall, me and you, what a night. I went home with bits of brick in me bum.
Scullery Ay well that was sometime ago Brenda, before you flopped.
Brenda Scullery, that night I felt I'd bin shot. (*She reaches up*)
Scullery Really?
Brenda Really. (*Up on her toes*)
Scullery (*reaching down*) Juliet.
Brenda (*jumping up*) Romeo.

He gets her arm, pulls her up a bit

You're the only man.

He gets her higher towards him

The only one.

Their faces nearly touching

Lend us a fiver.

He drops her

Scullery Flea Queen!
Brenda Up yours!
Scullery Come on, get in me sack. I'll weigh you in as rags!
Brenda (*going*) Aw fuck off!
Scullery Get tidy!
Brenda Piss off!

Brenda exits

Scullery (*to the audience*) Some ladies. (*He goes in to the house again. From inside*) What a mess and pong.

We hear him rummaging. He comes to the window, leans on the sill

How is it when, tell me this, when you goes in an auld empty house there's always an old doll (*he holds up a doll*), burnt paper (*he holds up a bit of burnt newspaper, looking at it*), and a Christmas card. (*He holds it up and lets it drop to the street*)

He goes back in. He comments on what he sees and what it's worth

Right, get picking the Road's bones. Old tap thirty p. (*He drops it in the sack*) Basket a bob. (*He drops it in*) Bit o' copper piping, one pound seventy. Crucifix. (*He looks at it closely*) They're no good without a Jesus. (*He chucks it*) A musical box! (*He picks up a little kid's dirty plastic musical box*) I'm having that. (*He shoves it in his special pocket. He comes out, throws the full pillow-case down to the street and clambers over the sill. As he's bringing his leg over*) Might have this bit of sack here. You never know. (*He rips it down and he drops to the ground. He starts stuffing the sacking into the pillow-case*)

Suddenly a big bald man appears at the same window, angry

Bald What the bloody hell's goin' on!

Scullery looks out to the audience. He looks slowly up to Bald

Scullery Sorry, I thought there was no-one living there.
Bald Well there bloody well is.

A woman's voice is heard from the back of the house

Mrs Bald What's up?
Bald Nowt just bin' robbed.
Mrs Bald Well kick him.
Bald I'll kick you in a minute. (*He turns to Scullery*) Here. Give us that.
Scullery (*slowly, reluctantly, passing the bag back*) Sorry.

Bald snatches it. Scullery passes up the Christmas card

Bald I don't want that.

   Bald goes in

Mrs Bald (*off, inside*) Are you coming back to bed?
Bald (*off, inside*) Shut it.

Scullery looks out to the audience in disbelief

Black-out

The Lights come up on an old armchair, ironing-board and iron. Jerry is polishing his shoes. He is middle-aged, soft-spoken, threadbare, with a big hole in his sock

Jerry I can't get over it. I can't get over the past how it was. I just can't. (*He puts his shoes down*) Oh God, I get these strong feelings inside and they're so sad I can hardly stand it. (*He puts his tie on the ironing board, irons it*) Oh, oh I can feel one now, it's breaking my heart with its strength and tears are coming in my eyes, and that's just because I thought of something from ago. Oh God. (*He gets down to ironing again*) Oh they were lovely lovely times though, and such a lilt to them, I go down it when I think. (*He sits down, looking up*) I hate to mention it, but that big silver ball turning there and all the lights coming off it on to us lot dancing below, and the big band there. And all the lads and girls I knew, all with their own special character. And the way you stood, you know, and you had a cigarette. You even lit a cigarette different then. There was some way, I can't do it now, good thing too, if I could I'd cry me flipping heart out. That's why I never wear Brylcream these days. I can't. National service too, you did. Everybody did it. You never complained much then, you never felt like complainin', I don't know why. National service though, you'd all be there. I was RAF, in that soft blue uniform, beret. (*He touches his head*) When you had a break you'd lie on your bunk, your mate might say, "Give us a tab". (*He puts his hands over his eyes*) And when you went on leave home. To your home town. The weather always seemed to be a bit misty and you'd be walking around familiar streets in your uniform. And everyone would have a little something to say to you. And you'd go to your girlfriend's factory. And they'd send up for her: "There's a man in uniform to see you." And you'd wait outside, take your cigs out your top pocket. (*He touches there*) Light up. Stand there in the misty weather, in your uniform. Full up with something. And everyone was an apprentice something. Serving your time. Or you could work for more money in the beginning in a warehouse or the railway, but it didn't pay off eventually. Or be a fly-boy and sell toys and annuals in the pubs. There was so many jobs then. A lot of people would start one in the morning, finish it, start another in the afternoon, finish it, and go in somewhere else the next day. You had the hit parade. Holidays in the Isle of Man or Blackpool. *Volarie.* We all felt special but safe at the same time. I don't know. You know I'm not saying this is right, but girls didn't even go in pubs. They didn't. At the dance, in the interval the lads all went in the pub next door. The girls stayed in the dance hall, then afterwards we all came back. And the girls, so pretty. Oh when I think of them. (*He puts his hands over his eyes*) And you went courting in them days, you courted. You walked with them and they had their cardigan over their arm. (*He puts his hand up to his face*) And the pictures. You went twice, three times a week. The stars, the music, black and white, the kissing. Sex, when I say the word now, and when I said it then it feels different in me. I know it sounds, you know, but it does. I can't get away from the past. I just can't. But no matter what they say. I can't see how that time could turn into this time. So horrible for me and so complicated for me. And being poor and no good, no use. (*He looks up, tears in his eyes*) I see 'em now me old friends, their young faces turning round and smiling. Fucking hell who's spoiling life, me, us, them or God.

Black-out

The sound of a dustbin lid falling down and shouting. The Lights come up on the Road

> *Scullery and Blowpipe burst in. Blowpipe is banging an empty beer crate on the floor and all about*

Scullery It's wrong! It's all fucking wrong! (*He shouts to the sky*) You fucking bastards!

Blowpipe flops out. Scullery kicks a dustbin flying

(*To Blowpipe*) That's me! (*To the audience*) That's me!

Blowpipe has picked up the dustbin lid and is banging it on the floor like a warrior. Scullery rips his coat off and faces the audience

Come on one at a time! I walk tall.

*He turns away, stares at Blowpipe. Blowpipe stops the banging. Scullery goes
and stands facing the wall. Silence. Then he turns to the audience, and bursts
out laughing*

Sorry about that mates. You've got to clear the system once in a while
an't you? Ha! Come on Blowpipe. (*He starts dusting him off*) Smarten
yourself up. Got get in for another pint soon.

Clare comes on, a young girl about sixteen

Clare Hello Scullery.
Scullery Hello Clare love. Where you goin'?
Clare To see Joey.
Scullery Oh ay.
Clare He's still not eating Scullery. Nowt for four days now.
Scullery Nowt? Not even a pie?
Clare No.
Scullery Bloody hell!
Clare I'm worried sick. What can I say to him, Scullery?
Scullery Fish chips pudding and peas.
Clare Scullery!

Scullery has a good laugh

Clare exits

Molly enters

Scullery (*seeing her*) Auld Molly. Gi' us a song.
Molly Gi' us a drink.
Scullery Blowpipe!

*Blowpipe gives her the bottle. She has a swig. Blowpipe tries to retrieve it.
Scullery knocks him down*

Get back.

Molly has finished her drink

Molly Reet. What do you want?
Scullery Owt.
Molly I'll sing you what I sang at one o' me weddings.

*Molly sings a beautiful old Lancashire folk song. She finishes. Blowpipe is
moved. The Lights dim. Molly comforts him*

Molly and Blowpipe exit

At the same time Scullery wheels out a bed from the shadows. He pushes it c
*and into a spotlight. In the bed is a young lad of about seventeen. Scullery
stands behind the bed-head and states strongly:*

Scullery "JOEY'S STORY."

He goes off

Darkness. A loud knocking starts. The knocking stops. Silence

Mother's voice (*off*) Joey come out! Come on out for Godsake. JOEY!!

Silence. The Lights come up. Joey is curled up in bed staring out

Joey I'm not lonely. I'm lying here now for four days. She keeps on trying to bring food in. I won't have none. I'm not to eat or drink. I'm on a diet since Wednesday. AND NO-ONE'S GONNA STOP ME!!

Pause

> They keep on a-knocking, keep on a-banging on the bastard door. But I won't answer. Because what's out there anyroad eh? They might as well put a sign over the door top here reading "Gents". Because out there is just a bog. The world's a fat toilet. It's true that, true as breath that little comment. True as trees . . . Fuck me, you babble when you've not eaten don't you? They're always a-falling out, your thoughts. You get a great brainful then your mouth sicks them out. This is what I'm seeking though. I want everything right out. Right the way out. This is why "I'm on the diet. Fuck me I'm dry. My throat's a bone. (*He looks all around him*) Fucking hell am I in a film or what? (*He laughs to himself*) Madhouse innit this nineteen eighty-seven. Packed with muck. There's no jobs. I was robbed of mine. My future snatched. A smash and grab job. I don't care now though. Bloody hell I'm knacked.

A loud knock on the door

Father's voice (*off*) Clare's here. Do you want to see her or not?
Joey Get stuffed.
Father's voice (*off*) You bloody little nutter!
Clare (*off*) No, Mr Cragg let me go in.

The door is unlocked. Joey goes right down under the blankets

> Clare comes in and closes the door

> Joey.

No reply

> Joey, come on love.

No reply. She goes over to touch him. He does a monkey impersonation. She screams

> Joey! What you doing?
Joey Nothing.
Clare Oh Joey, this isn't right. Why are you starving yourself? What's it for, everybody's worried sick for you. You can't just do this you know.
Joey Why not?
Clare Look we all feel like this sometime. But life must go on.
Joey Why?

Clare Eh? Oh don't be stupid. What about me, I've no job now either but I'm not behaving like a bloody big kid. Anyone can do that you know.
Joey Look if I'd wanted Marje Proops I would have writ' to the bitch. GO HOME!

Pause

Clare (*soft*) Joe.
Joey Can't you see this is something else, eh? Go on, get out.

Silence. Long pause

Clare I'd rather get in bed.

Silence. He looks at her. She takes her coat off. Then her top, then her skirt and gets in bed with him. He just keeps watching

Black-out

At this point, either a Black-out then Lights up to denote time passing, or the following speech:

> *Bisto the pub DJ enters with a pack of leaflets. (On them is something like, "Bisto and his Beatoven disco. Tonight at the Millstone Pub") He throws these out to the audience as he speaks. He wears a hat with two stuffed fingers on top in the V-sign*

Bisto How you doing? Okey dokey, I hopey so. I'm Bisto the foul mouthiest DJ you'll ever know. (*Catchphrase, he shoves two fingers up*) You'll get used to me. (*He points*) You'd better. Ha! When you've done here, why not come down to *Millstone Pub* and move up and down wi' BISTO and his BEATOVEN disco. (*He shoves two fingers up*) You'll get used to me. (*He points*) You'd better. I'm available for weddings, engagements, barmitzvahs, anything you like. I guarantee to get the most miserable cunt at the wedding up and dancing or your money back. You'll get used to me. You'd better.

> *He exits*

The Lights come up. Joey and Clare are sitting up in bed

Joey I said go home.
Clare No I'm staying with you. Anything you can do I can do better.
Joey (*pleased, yodelling*) OOOOOOOOOHHHHhhhhh!
Clare Are we protesting?
Joey I don't know love. Why are you here anyway?
Clare I don't know. I suppose I don't know what else to do. Every day's the same now. You were my only hobby really, now you're out of it, seems mad to carry on, all me ambition's gone. I filled in a *Honey* quiz last week. "Have you got driving force?" I got top marks all round. But where can I drive it, Joe? I lost my lovely little job. My office job. I bloody loved going in there you know. Well you do know, I told you about it every night. I felt so sweet and neat in there. Making order out of things. Being skilful. Tackling an awkward situation here and there. To have a destination. The

bus stop, then the office, then the work on the desk. Exercise to my body, my imagination, my general knowledge. Learning life's little steps. Now I'm saggy from tip to toe. Every day's like swimming in ache. I can't stand wearing the same clothes again and again. Re-hemming, stitching, I'm sick with it, Joe. I heard my mum cry again last night. My room's cold. I can't buy my favourite shampoo. Everybody's poor and sickly-white. Oh Joe! Joe! Joe!

Joey (*comforting her*) Never mind lovey. Never mind.

Clare Oh Joe I want to understand. Are we protesting?

Joey No, we're just ...

Clare Eh?

Joey Seeing what will take place in our heads.

Clare But we might die.

Joey We might not. We might have some secret revealed to us.

Clare Oh Joe.

Mother's voice (*from outside*) Your mum's on the phone Clare. She's worried, when are you going home?

No reply

      Clare.

Clare Tell her I'm on an adventure and not to worry!

Joey (*pleased*) Oh yes: (*He yodels*) OOOOOOOHHhhhhhhh! (*He kisses her*)

Mother's voice (*off*) Oh Clare. Oh.

She goes away. The sound of her going down steps

Clare I've never been so happy as the day we met you know.

Joey Go on. It was good though wun't it. I remember you pulled your T-shirt down a bit to show me your tan.

Clare Oh yeah I did.

Joey You were a right flirt then wun't you?

Clare No! That was the first time I'd ever done owt so brave.

Joey Yeah maybe, but you'd had it before 'an't you?

Clare Only once. With Gary Stones. On his couch when his mum was ill upstairs. I didn't like it much.

Joey I'm not surprised.

Clare What do you mean?

Joey He's like bad beef that bloke.

Clare Is he heck.

Joey Oh well go and have a pigging scene with him then!

Clare Oh.

Silence

      What about you then. You've had more than a few sexual what's-its-names before me, sexual adventures shall we say. According to what I've heard anyroad. What about her then, Jackie Snook. She's no starlet is she, more like a fartlet ... Looks like God give her an extra armpit to use as a mouth.

Joey Shut it.
Clare Uh.

Silence

Eh Joe, serious though, tell me about your first sex. You never have.
Joey Why?
Clare I told you.

No reply

Now we're together in this we should bring everything out.
Joey Well this is what I'm trying to do get everything out.
Clare Come on then.
Joey Yeah. Right then. OK, I was . . . I thought I'd told you this.
Clare No.
Joey OK. Me and Steve Carlisle went to the Nevada in Bolton, roller
skating, Thursday night, "The Brothel on Wheels". I was about fourteen
then. We were pretending to be French, talking to birds in the accent. This
girl was next to me an' I said " 'Ello you are verrry beootiful." She said
"You're not French you." I said "I ham, I ham." Anyway I kept it up for
about fifteen minutes, then admitted it wun't true, took her over the park
and fucked her up against a bulldozer wheel.
Clare Oh. And what was it like?
Joey Very muddy.
Clare Uh.
Joey Are you jealous now?
Clare Am I heck.

Joey gives a gentle laugh. Pause. Silence.

(*A thought strikes her*) Joe?
Joey Yeah.
Clare This what we're doing, is it 'owt to do with Phil Bott. Phil the
commie. Because he talks so fast I've never understood a word he's said
yet. Tell me no.
Joey No.

Pause

I tried all that for a bit. I went with Phil to his meetings, but still I cun'
decide who to attack. There's not one thing to blame. There's not just
good and bad, everything's deeper. But I can't get down there to dig out
the answer. I try. I try me bestest. I keep plunging meself in me mind but I
return empty-handed. I'm unhappy. So fucked off! And every bastard I
meet is just the same.

Silence. Clare tries to kiss him. He resists. Pause

Clare Joe, I'm getting hungry.

Pause

Joe.

He pulls the sheet back hard

Joey Go!
Clare No, Joe. No.
Joey Get out!
Clare No. (*She pulls the covers back up*)
Joey Well don't start, then.

Pause

Clare Why we doing this, Joe?
Joey I'm after something.
Clare What?
Joey How should I know? If I knew it I wun't be piggin' after it, would I?
Clare I don't understand you.
Joey Look there's summat missing. Life can't be just this, can it? What everybody's doing.
Clare That way madness lies.
Joey Eh?
Clare That's what my mum says. Any time there's any of that. Any clever talk on the telly she says it to us. She says just get on with it. Live your life and that's all there is to it.
Joey Oh?
Clare Well what does that mean?
Joey You're not serious. You're not even a joke. You're just like all the rest of them. Frightened to sniff the wind for fear it'll blow your brain upside down and then you'll (*he puts on a pathetic voice*) "have to do something different". Wasting your whole lives. Work, work, work, work, work. Small wages, small wages, small wages. Gettin' by with a smile. Gettin' by without a smile. Work, work, work, work. Small wages. Then death with the big "D". Not even a smell left over from it all. If you're lucky, a see-through memory, slowly dissolving like "Steradent".
Clare Don't insult my mum you!
Joey OH FOR FUCK'S SAKE, IS THAT ALL YOU CAN SAY?
Clare (*seeing he's out of control, trying to cool him*) Oh Joe. Come on. Bloody hell. I didn't mean nowt.
Joey EH!
Clare (*trying again*) I'm sorry, Joe. OK. Bloody hell. I mean bloody hell. Come on Joe. I didn't mean nowt when I said it. I mean this is not like you Joe.
Joey (*anger rising again*) UH.
Clare Now don't start, Joe. What I mean is you must admit you've not shown me this face before. I had no idea.
Joey (*coming round, a bit embarrassed*) Ay well, try having an idea now and again, eh. It don't hurt you know. Try, try it.
Clare (*faked laugh*) Eh, come on now. (*Pause. Silence. A bit afraid, quiet*) When did you start thinking like this, Joe?
Joey (*quietly*) When did I start? When did I stop's more like it! What the fuck's it all about Clare?! That's the one, that's the boy, that's putting the

head butt on my heart. You don't get the chance to find out. They rush
you from the cradle to the grave. But now we've come to a standstill, no
job, no hope, you've got to ask the question. You've got to ask. And it
does you fucking good, too.

Clare It don't look like it's done you much good. Lying there, half-dead.

Joey Come on love. What the fuck else is worth doing? (*He shoves his face
violently at hers*) EH?!!

She screams. Loud knocking starts on the door

He pulls her to him and kisses her with love

Black-out

They remain in bed onstage. The next scene occurs around them

The Lights come up on the Road

Scullery's tidying himself up. He's combing his hair in a small mirror

Scullery Have a good guess at me age, go on. (*He puts his comb away*) I'm
older than you think. Ha. (*He pulls his jacket together*) I was just thinking
there. How do we go about building a better future for our kiddies.

The Professor enters

Professor Scullery, Scullery.
Scullery Prof. Prof.
Professor Can I do a recollection of you?
Scullery Who me? No. Really? Go on then.

*The Professor turns the tape on, hands over the mike. The mike makes
Scullery feel like a night-club host*

Testing, one two, one two. I don't know where to start. I've had a long
life, some of it rough skin, some of it smooth. But on the "hole" I've
always gone down. I likes it that way. Thank you very much ladies and
gents, thank, thank you. I don't know what else I can say really but bless
the dark and all who scrape in her. And if you're driving home tonight
give us a lift you tight stink. And just remember folks if God did make
them little green apples he also made snot. Thank you. Thank.

*He has got the hang of it now and takes up the mike again. The Professor
hurriedly retrieves it*

Well that's worth a drink innit, Prof?
Professor (*putting the tape away*) Er well I . . .
Scullery You can give us a lift for that! Yeearrrr. (*He jumps on the
Professor's back*)

The Professor runs out, Scullery riding him

(*Laughing*) This is "Road" for you. This is "Road".

He laughs, laughing uproariously, as they exit

Black-out

The Lights come up on Joey's room. Two weeks later

Joey is sitting up in bed with his arm around Clare. She is sleeping. Joey's face really shows the strain now, it is taut and white

Joey I feel like England's forcing the brain out me head. I'm sick of it. Sick of it all. People reading newspapers: "EUROVISION LOVERS", "OUR QUEEN MUM", "MAGGIE'S TEARS", being fooled again and again. What the fuck-fuck is it? Where am I? Bin lying here two weeks now. On and on through the strain. I wear pain like a hat. Everyone's insane. The world really is a bucket of devil sick. Every little moment's stupid. I'm sick of people—people, stupid people. Frying the air with their mucky words, their mucky thoughts, their mucky deeds. Horrible sex being had under rotten bedding. Sickly sex being had on the waterbed. Where has man gone? Why is he so wrong? Why am I hurt all through? Every piece of me is bruised or gnawed raw, if you could see it, my heart's like an elbow. I've been done through by them, it, the crushing sky of ignorance, thigh of pignorance. What did I do! What was my crime? Who do I blame? God for giving me a spark of vision? Not enough of one, not enough of the other, just enough for discontent, enough to have me right out on the edge. Not able to get anyone out here with me, not able to get in with the rest. Oh God I'm so far gone it's too late. I'm half dead and I'm not sad or glad. I'm not sad or glad, what a fucking, bastard, bitching, cunt state to be in. I'm black inside. Bitterness has swelled like a mighty black rose inside me. Its petals are creaking against my chest. I want it out! Out! Out! Devil, God, devil, God, devil, God, save me something. Anything. There's got to be summat will come to help us. If only we can make the right state. If I can only get myself into the right state. This is it. This is why I'm on the diet. (*He looks around, remembering*) Fucking hell am I in a film or what? Or snot, or what. (*He is tightening*) IIIIIIIIIIIIIIII bring up small white birds covered in bile and fat blood, they was my hopes. I bring up a small hard pig that was my destiny. I'd like to bring it all out but bbbbbbbbbbbbut I've gone all constipated on bitterness, it won't remove itself. God give me a laxative if you got one. Ha! AArrrrrrgh! Arrrrrgh! Oh AAArrrrrrgh! (*He's sweating and straining*) Come out, come out, you tight bastard. Oh no! Death suck me up through that straw inside my spine! No leave me! Oh I'm full of dark frost. Who's done this to me! And why? Oh why? Is it worth that extra bit of business to see me suffer, is it? I blame you BUSINESS and you RELIGION its favourite friend, hand in hand YOU HAVE MUR-DERED THE CHILD IN MAN! MURDERERS! CUNTS! I'D LIKE TO CUT OPEN YOUR BELLIES AND SEE THE BROWN POUR!

It should appear that he's going to get out of bed to really kill somebody. Then Clare wakes. She puts her arm on him (For a shorter version of this ending please see p. 57)

Clare Joey.
Joey Eh?

Clare Joey, I feel so faint and white. I can hardly see my Joey.
Joey Don't worry about it. There might be a message or a sign soon.
Clare Uh?
Joey You never can tell when it's a going to come on you. Fuck me I wish I could sweat or something, I'm like paper.
Clare I'm empty and dried-out too, it's so weird now Joe. (*Silence*) Joe, is my skin cracking?
Joey No.
Clare Around my mouth at the corners is there any cracking?
Joey (*a quick glance*) No.
Clare It feels like it is.

> *Clare starts to sing to herself, very softly, a verse from* Wonderful World *(Sam Cooke/Herb Alpert/Lou Adler). She stops. Silence*

Silence

I love you so much, Joey.
Joey Eh?
Clare I love you, my man. Perhaps if I cried you could drink up my tears.
Joey Be quiet now.
Clare It feels right funny. I can feel things very fine with my body now. Very fine like the silence within silence within silence. Joey is it death-time?
Joey (*shocked*) Stop it! You're talking now like you've never talked in your life.
Clare Where's it coming from?
Joey You! You!
Clare Who?
Joey Oh no. You're more advanced now than me. You're going somewhere. A state. Into a state.
Clare Eh?
Joey Are you in a trance or what?
Clare I don't know.
Joey Just shout out things. That's how I'll test you. Just say things what come into your head.
Clare How can a? A can't hardly speak.
Joey What do you mean?
Clare I'm so knackered out. A feel I'm just holding on by the threads. One or two fine wet threads, the rest have dried an' broke.
Joey Oh my dear.
Clare Don't worry. I still love you, that's left. I keep on seeing faces, like me dad's, me mum's, me dad's again. I still want to cry when I see me dad's dismantled face. He lost his last job you know. Just think one day there might be the last job on earth. And everyone will come out to see the man lose it. They'll all watch as he comes up to his last hour. The last hooter blow whoooooooooooo oh ooooooo ooooooooooo oooooo I'm being corny now, int a Joey? Oh my it's white in here behind the eyes, so misty.

She closes her eyes. Joey holds her. He makes a fist. He shakes it at the audience. He shakes it up at the sky. He shakes it at the door where the family are outside. He shakes it down under the bed. Then he puts it in front of his face and bites into his hand

Black-out

The Lights come up
Clare is lying down one side of the bed. He's covered up her face. He is now the other way round, lying with his feet on the pillow, his head hanging over the edge. He sees the audience upside down, his eyes staring up, his mouth wide open. He makes a noise in his throat.

Joey Gaaaaraaaaa   ga   gaaaaaaaaarr   gaaaa   aaaaa.   Ga.   Ga. agraaaaaaaaaaaaa ga. Gaaaaaaaaa aaa. Ga ga. Smart in' it? Smart arse innit? To end back to front on the bed. Look at me. I am pain. I am now from tip to toe. Look at me I am the solution. There is no solution. How about that then. That's the smart—arsest simplest answer going. The last answer to the first question. There is no solution. (*He stops and stares*) But you're all adding a "maybe" aren't you. (*He winks then dies*)

From out of the shadows Scullery comes over. He takes the sheet and covers Joey's face.

Scullery (*to the audience*) Hey we's gonna miss last orders. I's have to see Girly, then I'll get in there with you. I'll just step back into the dark. (*He starts stepping back*) See you soon.

The Lights fade to Black-out

INTERVAL

A development of the Royal Court promenade production was a disco in the theatre and entertainment in the bar during the interval. If this interval section is not used then the chip shop scene in Act 2 should also be cut, so that the 2nd half opens with Scullery and the musical box and then moves immediately to the 3rd scene where Dor and Lane appear high up eating chips

The two scenes run at the same time: disco in the theatre, pub in the bar. The bar scene begins later and ends earlier to give people time to get in and out and return to the disco for the floor show. Acts in the pub can be anything the actors choose

The Disco

After the Black-out at the end of Act I, the Lights come up a little. A pause to establish the interval. Then a burst of light and music. The stage has become a disco, up behind a flashing record deck is Bisto

Bisto Welcome to *Millstone Pub*. I'm Bisto. And this is the Beatoven Disco.
You'll get used to me . . . You'd better. By my calculatours we've only got
fifteen minutes till last orders, so let's dance!

*Madonna or any full dance sound up to full. After a minute, if enough people
don't go through to the bar, Madonna down to half, under:*

I've just had a call through from the bar saying where the fuck is
everybody. There's a turn coming on in a minute, so go and drink or stay
and dance.

*Madonna up to full. Madonna into the Bee Gees' "Saturday Night Fever"
under the intro:*

Come on, the floor is yours, so grab a mug and cut the rug, take your feet
and mash the beat, slide out there and show some flare, in other words,
dance you buggers!

Bee Gees up to full. Bee Gees fade under:

Ah the Bee Gees, great bunch of lads. Right. Have we any rockers in
tonight, ay rock and roll. Now I defy any bastard not to dance to this next
delight . . . the Teddy Boys' treat . . . a fifties' classic . . ." RED HOT
BOLLOCKS". . . oh sorry . . . "GREAT BALLS OF FIRE!!!!!"

"Great Balls of Fire" (Jerry Lee Lewis) comes straight in. When it ends:

That's what you can expect from Bisto. Music to dance to, talk through,
an' grab a slag to. All your favourite tunes an' flashing fucking lights an'
all. This next one is one o' me personal favourites, and I dedicate it to . . .
well you know who you are, ya bitch!

"Can't Get Used to Losing You" (Andy Williams) fades up to full

Meanwhile, in the bar . . .

Once a fair amount of audience are in, the compère gets onstage

Tom Stanley Ladies and gents, ladies and gents, can we have a bit of hush
an' order for a sec. Thank you. As you know, tonight is turn night here in
the old *Millstone Pub*, and we've got someone really special in tonight.
I'm sure you'll join me in welcoming Chance Peterson, ladies and gents.
Chance. Thank you.

*Chance comes on. He stands onstage, guitar round neck, sings a bit, then
collapses against the back wall*

I must apologize for this, ladies and gents. That's the last fucking time
we'll have him. In a way, it's dropped us in the muck. Anyway, er. I know.
I know. Anyone in the audience like to come up here on our famous stage
an' give us a song or summat? (*He peers out*) Is there anybody out there?
Ha.

Scullery steps forward and onstage

Scullery!

Scullery sings to a taped accompaniment

Tom Stanley returns

Tom Stanley Thank you ladies an' gents, could I ask you all to drink up now as last orders is gone. I don't mean to be unkindly. But shut up, sup up and shove off. May I say if you rush it you might catch the erotic dancers in our disco room.

Meanwhile, in the disco ...

"Can't Get Used to Losing You" (Andy Williams) plays, ends

Bisto Right now. We have a special thrill for you tonight. We've got live entertainment, when I say live I mean wild, when I say wild I mean red hot, when I say red hot I mean a right fucking turn on. That TITilating Trio, the exotic, erotic, you'll never believe your eyes, or their thighs, the breast in the land—THE ELECTRIC CLUTCH! THAT'S SHEENA ...

She runs on

That's TINA ...

She runs on

That's MAUREENA!

She runs on

This is sex.

They dance. It goes wrong—one of the girls does her back in. The others carry her off

What a fuck up, and I thought we were in for a bit of minge as well. Never mind. Right now it's time for the last song of the evening. It's a smooch, and as is customary at this time, Bisto asks you to glance around the room. There must be someone out there you've seen tonight and thought should I, could I. Well you can. Go on. Go over, take his or her hand, and just dance yourselves together. Beautiful. I want to thank each and every one of you for coming down tonight, and just remember. I love you, we love you, so you love you too, you're worth it, people. (*Soft and slow*) You'll get used to me. You'd better.

"Je T'aime" (Jane Birkin) up to full

Scullery gets people from the audience up onstage to dance together. Bisto comes down to help. Lane and Dor come in and get up partners. A drunken young Soldier comes onstage. Standing, wobbling, holding a woman's coat and bag. Helen (a middle-aged woman) comes through the crowd to find him, takes her coat and bag, leads him off. The dance continues until the record ends

ACT II

A spotlight picks out Scullery above. He puts his music box on. It plays "When You Wish Upon a Star". He dances to it. It finishes, he exits

The Lights come up as a chip shop is opened in the corner by Manfred the owner, and his assistant, a Scots Girl

Dor and Lane go over

Manfred What you havin' girls?
Lane Whooo don't ask her that.
Dor Have you got a sausage.

Lane laughs

Serve it up love.
Scots Girl Do you want chips?
Lane Ay the noo.
Dor She's Scottchish
Lane I know.
Dor Any haggis there?

While Dor and Lane are paying the girl . . .

Helen and the Soldier come up

Helen Two please. Chips and fish and pudding and chips. Gravy please. (*She sees the girl. She moves the Soldier to the other side*)

Helen and the Soldier exit after buying their chips

Manfred (*to the audience*) Come on now. CHIPS FISH. MUSHY PEAS. PUDDING. SPECIALS. MEAT PIES. CHEESE AND ONION PIES. SAUSAGE BATTERED OR NOT. BURGER. CHICKEN. BLACK PUDDING. FISHCAKE. BARM CAKES.

Scots Girl (*shouting*) The vans haven't come!
Manfred Oh. LADIES AND GENTS WE'VE GOT CHIPS. LOADS OF CHIPS. LONG CHIPS SHORT CHIPS. CHIP CHIPS. COME AN' GET'EM WHILE THEY'RE HOT BLEEDING CHIPS. (*To the girl*) Fucking hell. It would happen tonight when we's got a road full. I could a made me bastard fortune tonight. COME ON LOVE. CHIPS ARE HERE. THE LOVELIEST IN THE LAND. (*He holds one up*) LOOK AT THAT NORTHERN BEAUTY. IT'S THE LENGTH AND THE DEPTH AND THE LACK OF GREASE THAT MAKES IT WHAT IT

IS. (*He swallows it*) WHAT A VINTAGE. DON'T MISS THEM LOVE.
COME AND BUY . . .

The Lights cross-fade to . . .

Dor and Lane appear high up eating chips

Lane It were packed in there tonight weren't it?

Dor Too many drinkers an' not enough doers.

Lane What about Barry? I thought you was in.

Dor He's staying after time.

Lane Why don't we?

Dor I don't fancy it.

Lane What we gonna do now—no fellahs, no money. I'm not going home
to *him*.

Dor I'm not going home to *him*. God I feel a bit wuzzy I always do when
I'm standing still. (*She puts her hand out and leans on the wall*)

Lane Eh. What was up with him tonight?

Dor Who?

Lane Teddy.

Dor Teddy behind the bar?

Lane Ay old long face. He never even let on.

Dor I know, I know. And we were close at one time you know. He give me
and me cousin one once behind the pub.

Lane They're all the bastard same. God I wish you hadn't mentioned sex, I
feel naughty now.

Dor I do. (*She has a coughing fit*)

Lane Get it up.

Dor I wish somebody would.

Lane Ohhhhhhhhhhh. (*Indicating the audience below*) Well take your pick
Lane love. Yoo hoo.

Dor (*choosing someone who resembles a celebrity*) What about Blake
Carrington down there then.

Lane Come on.

They rush off as though to go for him

Scullery crosses eating chips

Scullery Last orders is gone. Everybody's coming home a bit pissed. Piping
hot these. (*He eats*)

Scullery exits

A young lad, Curt, staggers on, chips in hand. He grabs hold of a lamp-post

Curt God I feel sick. God I'm frightened if I just turn, it'll be too much.
God in here (*he touches his side*) there's too much floating, too much. I'm
not s'pose to drink with what I'm on, but I don't bother now. Enjoy what
you can, while you can, if you can can. (*He sniffs*) God it stinks in this
road. (*He sniffs*) Staleness, rot, sick, sex, drink, blood. There's always
been something wrong down here. It's where things slide to but don't

drop off. Even darkness is different down here, it's all red and black like blood and ink, and you feel it in the throat. I'm ill. (*He starts coughing*) Oh God I fell like I'm gonna throw. I don't wanna though (*He wraps his arms tight round the post and holds on, clenching his teeth as though something's passing over him. He stops, looks out again*) When you've been down for so long, under so much, you get like a pressed leaf, and stay that way for ever. Brown, sick-white, and flat. Aw. (*He lets go with one arm and lets himself swing*) Aw I'm sick of moaning. Be full of good cheer, if not then bad beer. (*He taps his stomach*) There you go.

He throws his chips high in the air. They scatter everywhere. He goes off

Black-out

Darkness except for a spotlight on an armchair C. *The Soldier is sitting in it, very drunk, staring out front. The spotlight breaks out over the stage. He turns to see the door open, an Alsatian dog crosses the room and goes out through the opposite door*

> *Then Helen backs in with two plates. One has chips, pudding and peas on it, one fish and chips. She shuts the door with her bum and goes over to him*

Helen Here they are love. I've put 'em on plates. Now which is which? Hang on. You're pudding that means I'm fish. Watch the gravy love it's dripping off one side.

She gives it to him, lays it on his knees. She drags a pouffe in the shape of a tortoise, over to the side of the armchair and sits by him. Her suspenders show

They make a nice chip at the chinky don't they? Bit greasy. Bet you miss this in the mess? Where's your camp anyway? You never said. You don't say much do you? Take your boots off if you like. Do you want the telly on? Well yes or no? Ooooh, you're the real quiet type aren't you? Still waters run deep or what? The Clint Eastwood type. Little mini Clint. Eh, I like him though do you? I like loners. That's why I sent Maureen to fetch you over tonight. That uniform, dead romantic. It's ages since I've seen a soldier. You just sort of stood out in the crowd. Would you kill somebody if you had to? Say they provoked you. That's your duty though in' it? This is what you get paid for. Licence to kill. You must have a laugh though. All this one-armed combat and what not. (*She sees something in her meal*) What the bloody hell's this? It's either mine or that bloody dog's. I'll skin the beast. Kojak! Kojak! Come 'ere. Look at that.

She holds it up in front of his face, a chip dangling on a long hair. He throws up into his meal. She gets up

Oh bloody hell. Oh heck.

She puts her chips down and goes off into the kitchen. The dog comes back on and starts eating her chips and fish. She comes back in with an old dirty towel

Kojak you bastard! Get out of it! (*She shoos the dog off with the towel*)
You bloody dirty git.

The Soldier looks up all lost and bleary

Not you cocker, him, that hound. (*She looks at him and the mess*) Oh dear.
Not to worry. (*She gets down and starts padding up the sick with the towel*)
I've got a flannel here cock. Let's just wipe your chops off.

*She wipes his face like a baby. He fights a bit in his drunken stupor like a baby
might. She pauses a moment in her wiping*

Aaaaw. (*She looks again, wipes on. She starts to loosen his tie*) Look, it's
all over your shirt and down your nice smart jacket. We can't have that
can we now. Eh? No we cannot. (*She starts to unbutton his jacket. At first
she's brisk and fast, then she slows down almost enjoying it. She pauses in
thought. She gets up and goes over to the record player by the bed. It's on
the floor, an old-fashioned mono-portable with a heavy arm. She picks a
record up. The records are without sleeves just in a pile on the floor. Some
are in an old wire record rack. She squats as she puts it on. As she gets it on
and the automatic begins and it drops, she falls over*) Oh bloody hell. (*She
giggles. As she lies there she looks up at him*)

*The music starts (Barry Manilow or Frank Sinatra). She gets up and walks
over to him. Now as she undresses him, the music has affected her, and she does
it seductively. She gets the jacket and shirt off. She looks again at the Soldier.
She kisses him, very sloppy and round*

Oh you are naughty. And so young as well. So young and full of it. I bet
you've had loads of girls already 'ant you eh? (*She kisses him again*) Why
should you choose me eh? (*She gets his cheeks in her hands*) Eh? Why?
What have I got? (*She puts her tongue in his ear*) Oh you sexy bugger.
Watch it. You really know what to do don't you? Not like most blokes. I
bet you're the type that knows how to cherish a girl. (*She hugs him and
puts her head on his chest*) So firm. I imagine you've got the girls running
round you like flies on muck. Why me? You could have your pick any
time. (*She touches his mouth with her fingers*) You could have your pick
even of the famous stars. (*She kisses him again, she shifts position, she
kneels in her plate of chips*) Oh. (*She looks at him*) Oh I am sorry I've
kneeled in my chips. Forgive me. (*She stands up, picks chips off her tights
and drops them on the plate. She picks the plate up and goes over to put it on
the sideboard. She sees the bed. She lies back on it in a sexy pose looking at
him*) Come on then. Oh you, you do play it cool. You know how to hold
back and get a woman sexed. (*She looks at him*) I know what we'll do.
(*She rolls over and changes the record*) I know. Just the job this one. Just
the blinking job.

*It starts blurting out. It's James Brown "Sex Machine". She turns it up even
louder. She rolls about a bit*

Wheeeeeeeee. (*She goes over to him, arms outstretched*) What you're gonna tak' me now. Just like that out of the blue. Bloody soldiers. (*She grabs him up off the chair and holds him close*) Oh. Oh. What you doing. Oh. Oh. Lover boy. Soldier of love.

They wobble back over to the bed

Wow, you've been overseas haven't you. What a touch boy. Wowie.

She flops back on the bed, letting him go. He just falls on top of her, she wraps her legs round him quick

Oh. Oh.

He slides off her into the record player and out on the floor. The music stops. She leans off the bed and over him

Are you all right? (*She comes out of it a bit. She runs her finger over his face*) You're like a little boy. (*She starts crying*) I'm sorry. Oh dear.

She cries more. She gets up and puts a pillow under his head and a blanket over him, then sits on the armchair drying her eyes

I don't know what they think you are. They treat you like last week's muck. (*She looks like she's going to cry again. She closes her eyes and gently shakes her head*) I feel right ashamed now. And so sad. (*She whispers it*) So sad. (*She says it voicelessly*) So sad. (*She closes her eyes and puts her head back*)

Black-out

Back to the Road

Blue light, spinning lights going round and round from a silver ball. Music playing: "The Last Waltz" (Engelbert Humperdinck). It's like in a dance hall of the fifties

Jerry comes on in a worn blue velvet jacket, shirt, tie. He is drunk and weepy-looking, eyes closed, dancing round and round with himself, across the stage

Scullery appears, eating his last chip

He quickly screws up the chip papers in a ball and throws them at Jerry. They bounce off his head. The music stops, the Lights go

Jerry strolls off, lost

Black-out

Scullery exits

The Lights come up. Dor is sitting on a bench. From above the sound of a woman (Mrs Bald) singing "Somewhere Over the Rainbow"

Bald (*off*) Shut it.

Silence

Barry enters. He has a pool cue. Drunk he takes a few pots and can involve one of the audience in a game

Barry (*to the audience*) Pool King me.
Dor Barry.
Barry (*looking round*) How you doing? Do you fancy a bit?
Dor Not at the moment.
Barry Got a light?

Dor strikes a match for him

> *Above, Bald's face is squashed against the glass*

Bald Put that light out!

They both look up

> *He's gone*

Barry What's up anyroad?
Dor I've lost me bastard keys. I'm locked out.

Barry laughs

> Help me find 'em.
Barry No way. (*He pulls a bottle of beer out of each pocket*) Have you got an opener?
Dor There's one on me key-ring.
Barry (*jumping up*) You look there! I'll look here!

As they search, they speak to the audience

Dor You seen a key?
Barry Seen a key love?

Barry goes down on all fours and can't be seen

> *Bald opens the window*

Bald Hey what you looking for?
Dor A key.
Bald Well fuck off then!
Dor Shove it you miserable old crow.
Bald You what! What did you say!!!
Barry (*suddenly standing*) She said shut your stink hole fat face!
Bald (*meekly*) Oh I see I just wondered. Bye.

> *He goes back in*

Barry (*holding the bottles out*) Where's this opener? (*Up to the window*) Oy you! Oy Rambo! Have you got opener!

The window opens and Bald appears

Bald (*a tirade*) What do you think this is eh! Keeping decent ones awake like this. My wife's awake here.
Mrs Bald I'm not.

Bald You are! It's bloody disgusting. Hey and I know your husband.
Dor So do I.
Bald Shouting up the road. Drunks. Hooligans . . . *etc. etc.*
Barry (*shouting over the noise*) Hey. Hey. I'll tell you what. Deal. Opener for a bottle.

Bald suddenly stops shouting. He goes in

An opener comes out, hits the ground

Barry picks it up. He motions to Dor. They go. Bald appears at the window with his special tankard

Bald Hey hey what about deal!?

They can be heard laughing off-stage

Bald looks out, goes in

Mrs Bald (*off*) Sucker.
Bald (*off*) Shut it.
Mrs Bald (*off*) He he he.

Black-out

The Lights come up on a woman waiting, smoking. She is in her mid-thirties, sitting on a hard kitchen chair. She has a scruffy dressing-gown on, a bit of sad nightie showing

Valerie I'm fed up of sitting here waiting for him, he'll be another hundred years at his rate. What a life, get up, feed every baby in the house. Do everything else I can, without cash. While he drinks, drinks it, drinks it, and shoves nothing my way except his fat hard hands in bed at night. Rough dog he is. Big rough heavy dog. Dog with sick in its fur. He has me pulling my hair out. Look at my hair, it's so dry. So sadly dried. I'd cry but I don't think tears would come. And there's nothing worse than an empty cry. It's like choking. Why do we do it? Why do I stay? Why the why why? You can cover yourself in questions and you're none the wiser 'cause you're too tired to answer. Always scrimping and scraping. He just takes the Giro and does what he wants with it. Leaves a few pounds on the table corner sometimes, sometimes. But you never know when and if you ask him he chops you one. That's why I have to borrow, borrow off everyone. I am like a bony rat going here, going there, trying to sniffle something out. They help me, though I'll bet you they hate me really. Despise me really. Because I'm always there an' keep asking, asking and they can't say no. They just open their purses, and I says, thank you, thank you a thousand times till we all feel sick. God I can't wait till the kids are older then I can send them. He'll come in soon. Pissed drunk through. Telling me I should do more about the place. Eating whatever's in the house. Pissing and missing the bog. Squeezing the kids too hard. Shouting then sulking. Then sleeping all deep and smelly, wrapped over and over in the blankets. Drink's a bastard. Drink's a swilly brown bastard. A smelling stench sea. And he's the captain with his bristles wet through. Swallowing and throwing, swallowing and throwing white brown water all over me. Oh what am I saying, it's a nightmare all this. I blame him then I don't blame him. It's not his fault there's no work. He's such a big man, he's nowhere to put himself. He looks so awkward and sad at the sink, the vacuum's like a toy in his hand. When he's in all day he fills up the room. Like a big wounded animal, moving about, trying to find his slippers, clumsy with the small things of the house, bewildered. I see this. I see the poor beast in the wrong world. I see his eyes sad and low. I see him as the days go on, old damp sacks one on top of another. I see him, the waste. The human waste of the land. But I can't forgive him. I can't forgive the cruel of the big fucking heap. The big fucking clumsy heap. (*She startles herself with what she's saying, nearly cries*) He's so big and hunched and ugly. (*Holding back*) Oh my man. (*She chokes*) I hate him now, and I didn't used to. I hate him now, and I don't want to. (*She cries*) Can we not have before again, can we not? (*She cries*) Can we not have before again. (*She looks out manic and abrupt*) Can we not?

Black-out

> *The sound of Chantal's song. The Lights come up as she appears still singing to herself, toying with a cigarette. (This next bit should be improvised around who she sees etc., etc.) She flirts with men in the audience*

Chantal (*to a man*) Have you got a light? (*She moves on to another man, sings a bit*) Have you got one Smiley? (*She moves on*) Have you got a light?

She likes this one. She goes over to him, plays with his tie, leads him off by it to the nearest exit. As they go . . .

> *Bald appears*

Bald (*from the window above*) CHANTAL! CHANTAL!
Chantal What!
Bald Get in. Your mother's worried.
Mrs Bald I'm not.
Bald You are!

> *Chantal carries on out with the man*

> *Bald disappears*

Black-out

Back to the Road

> *Scullery comes on pissed and staggering*

Scullery Blowpipe! Blowpipe! Blowpipe! Blowpipe!

> *Blowpipe appears*

Where you bin? (*He smacks him on top of his cap*)
Blowpipe Rustling. (*He pulls out a full bottle of unopened rum*)
Scullery (*taking it*) Ah my saviour. (*He kisses him. He kisses the bottle. He holds it out to the audience at arm's length*)

He links arms with Blowpipe and they set off

As they go off they pass a drunk woman (Marion) coming on with Brian

Marion Scullduggery!
Scullery Marion!

Brian pulls at her

Where you goin'?
Marion Being brushed off my feet.

They go off on the other side from Scullery and Blowpipe

The Lights come up on a living-room

Marion and Brian come in really pissed. She flops on the couch. He stands over her, pulls his zip down

Marion (*pushing him away*) No I want a butty first.
Brian (*indicating the kitchen*) Well there's some bloody luncheon meat in there. Get one.
Marion Bloody hell. Bloody hell eh, can't even mak' us summat eat now.
Brian Arrgh.

She stumbles into the kitchen

He goes over to sideboard and gets a bottle of sherry out. She screams. He drunkenly stumbles round.

She comes in, blood dripping all over her thumb

Marion I cut me bleeding thumb.

He stumbles over to her, gets hold of her all lovey, puckering his lips in sympathy

Get off. (*She goes to the couch, to her handbag, opens it, drops it*) Sodding hell. (*She gets a tissue out, holds it on*)

He comes over and sits next to her on the couch, puts his arm round her. They let their heads drop together. They talk drunkenly, like two babies

Brian How my likkle luv.
Marion Thumb.
Brian Naughty thumb.
Marion It's sore.
Brian Aawwwwww. Cum here.

He holds her, kisses her, catches her thumb

Marion Owwww. Get off!

She pushes him off. He lies back on the couch. She does also

Give us a swig.

He gives her the bottle, stands up, burps, takes it back

Eh eh, I've not finished yet. (*She grabs at it*)

Brian You don't think you're having all me drink and not giving us a shag do you?

Marion (*snatching the drink off him*) I don't tease a man me. No way. I wouldn't give you a jack on then leave you. Come on Brian you know me better than that. (*She swigs it*) Get us a glass anyroad. Where's your manners.

She rubs herself up against him. He's so pissed he nearly falls over

Brian (*laughing*) Ha ha. Ay.

He goes in the kitchen

She has another swig, pulls her bra straight

He comes back with a big pint glass, gives it to her

She doesn't seem to bother, just pours drink in it. Both are still standing, tottering

Marion Where's your daughter?

He motions upstairs, puts his head on his hands; he means sleeping. Marion drinks. She falls back on the couch

Put a record on.

He walks stiff-legged over to the record player and puts Country and Western on very loud

(*Approving*) Hey hey. (*She lifts the glass*)

He comes back over to her, gets on the couch, starts holding her, kissing the side of her cheek big and round. She turns round, grabs his head, starts snogging him hard

The door opens and a girl comes in, about twelve, long hair, night-gown. She stops

They look at her. She looks at them

Linda I can't sleep for all t'noise, Dad.

Marion Is this her Brian? Well, she's bloody gorgeous, bloody gorgeous, her.

Brian Ay she's a good 'un.

Marion Come here, love.

The girl reluctantly comes over to the back of the settee. Marion kneels up on the couch, gets the girl's head and kisses her. The girl is trying to pull back

Lovely.

Blood goes on the girl's face from Marion's thumb. The girl touches it, looks at her father

What's up cock? Oh that's mine, off here. (*She shows her thumb*) The pig did it, him. (*She slaps him, playful*) Not making me nowt to eat. Come and sit down here love. Me neck's going (*She grabs her hand and drags her round and between them both*) Hold on. (*She goes in her bag and pulls out a tissue, spits on it and starts wiping the girl's face*) There you are cock. Eh don't be scared. Eh. (*She puts her arm round her*) Brian, turn that bleeding music down or off or summat, for me an' her. We don't like it loud do we. (*She is taking the girl's hair back behind her ear*) Eh not.

The girl looks miserable. Brian does turn the music down. He goes, pick up the bottle, swigs from it

Brian (*to Marion*) Come on upstairs.

Marion Hold your horses. We're talking here. What do you want to be when you grow up love?

The girl shrugs

Well whatever it is love, stick at it and you'll get there.

Brian grabs Marion's shoulder

Brian Come on now.

She knocks his hand off

Marion Who's your favourite pin-up star, love? Do you like them Agadoo?

He pokes her

Eh! (*To the girl*) Men.

The girl looks upset. He pokes her again

Brian Come on.
Marion Hang on.

He pokes her

No.

She looks to the girl. She's crying. Marion puts her arm round her. The girl slips free

Aw love, Aw. Cheer up cock. (*She turns to Brian, angry with him*) Here you. Put fucking Agadoo on for her. (*She shoves him towards the record player*)

He stops half-way

Brian I'm going.

He sets off for the door. He goes out, leaving door open, then goes out the front door

Marion Hey hang on. (*To the girl*) Miserable swine he is. Hey come back.

She gets up and goes out the door. The front door slams, off

The girl picks up the bottle off the floor and collects the tissues up. She straightens the couch up, turns to exit. On her way, she stops, turns back

Linda (*to the audience, mocking*) POOR LITTLE ME! (*She sticks her tongue out*)

She exits

A rattling is heard getting louder and louder. Suddenly Scullery enters pushing a shopping trolley at mad speed across the stage

Scullery Ayeeeeeeeeeeeeeeeee! (*He turns it and comes back to* C) Ayeeeeeeeeeeeeee!

As this happens, Brian comes on pursued by Marion (A shorter version of this row is on page 58)

Marion Come here you!
Brian Aw piss off!
Marion What's the fucking big idea?!
Brian Aw fuck off, woman!
Marion I'll fuck nowhere. You stand still!

Scullery is enjoying this. He sits in the trolley to watch

Brian Go with your little friend.
Marion Oh you nasty-minded bugger!

She grabs him, makes him stop. They end up on each side of the trolley, Scullery smack in the middle

You're a selfish bastard you, Brian. Me myself an' I! Me myself an' I.
Brian Aw fuck off.
Marion You know what your pissing problem is don't you eh?
Brian What?
Marion You don't know how to treat a woman.
Brian You know what your pissin' problem is don't you?
Marion What!
Brian You're not woman, you're tart.

She loses her temper more, goes for him, but he spins the trolley round between them. Now they're on opposite sides to before

Marion FART!
Brian TART!

Madder still at this, she gives chase again. Again he spins round putting the trolley between them

Marion (*can't get at him*) Arrrrrrgh!

Brink and Eddie appear in the gallery

Brink Where they gone?
Eddie Don't know, they said wait here a minute.
Brink (*seeing the row*) Look at that!
Eddie Come on!

They set off down

Onstage Brian leaves

Marion Eh come back you! I've not finished wi' you!

She goes off after him. They run through the theatre

Brian Away woman!
Marion No way!
Brian Piss off out of it!
Marion No way! No way! You lousy dick!
Marion Stop still! STOP STILL! STOP!
Brian Are you fucking mental altogether?
Marion You will be if I fuckin' clouts ya!
Brian Silly cow!
Marion What was that? What was fucking that! HOLD STILL YOU, YOU BASTARD!

They exit

Carol and Louise enter onstage. They hear the shouting

Carol Whats goin' on?
Louise Oh bloody hell fire.
Carol What's goin' on Scull?
Scullery Fight night. (*His hands to his mouth*) Dong dong seconds away round two.

Brian and Marion appear on the circle

Marion I'll kill you, Brian. I'll kill! I'm not joking.

Brink and Eddie appear in the circle

Brink Go on, Love!
Eddie Give him one!
Marion Piss off! OR YOU'LL PISSIN' GET IT!
Brink Promises.

She swings for him with her handbag. Eddie goes up behind her, slaps her backside. She hits him with her bag

Marion Prick!

From below

Carol (*shouting up*) Eh!
Louise Eh!
Carol Come down lads!
Louise Come down.
Scullery Stay up!

Louise hits him

Carol You're like bloody big kids, leave her!

Marion comes forward and leans over to shout down

Marion Oh listen little madam there. I can fight me own fucking battles, thank you!

Brink and Eddie crack up laughing at this

Carol You slag!
Louise You bloody fat slag!
Marion Aw fuck you.
Carol Watch it woman!
Louise Old slut!
Marion (*spits*) Piss off, young bitches.
Brian What a state to be in.
Marion You what! This is your cunting fault all this! Get here now!
Eddie Eh you're lovely when you're angry!
Marion Fuck off shrimp!
Brink What a lady.
Marion Don't push it, boy!
Brink I wun't push nowt in you, lovey.
Marion You young cunt. (*She goes for him*)
Scullery Get in there!
Louise Ignore her an' come down!
Carol Come on!
Louise Come on!
Carol Leave the old bag!

Brian leaves

Scullery There he goes love!
Marion (*turning round*) Eh eh come back, Brian. Come back!

She goes after him

The lads come down on stage

Carol Where've you two been. I thought you were waiting for us.
Brink Well, we're here now.

Scullery is still in the shopping trolley

Scullery Hey I'm on special offer; don't miss your bargain, girls.

Carol and Louise look at each other, smile, grab the trolley and shove him off

Scullery (*as he goes*) OOOhhhhhhhhhhhhhhhhhhhhhhhhhhhhhhhhhhh.

Marion and Brian appear at the very top gallery in spotlights

Marion You've shown me up tonight 'an't you! eh! You fat arsed twat.
Brian Get home cow!
Marion Never, you cunt!
Brian Get home!
Marion BRIAN! BRIAN! THE BASTARD BLEEDING FUCK!

Black-out

Brink and Eddie and Carol and Louise go towards Brink's place

The Lights come up on Brink's place. A long settee, two chairs, a massive stereo speaker, like bands have, in the corner; by it, a flat record deck; on the wall, hung by a gold nail, is a single record

> *Eddie enters first; he has five bottles of wine in his arms. He unloads them all on the end of the long settee. Brink enters. Then Carol and Louise come in together, giggling*

Eddie Take a seat girls, I'll get some glasses.
Carol Why, can you not see?

The girls both giggle

Eddie Eh?

They giggle again

> *Eddie shrugs, smiles and goes in the kitchen*

Brink Come on have a seat. (*To the audience, if promenade*) You too.

> *Brink goes off into the kitchen*

The girls walk around the settee together to front C. They stand looking around. They look at each other and start giggling again

Eddie (*off, from the kitchen*) Just tryin' to find a cork-screw!
Carol That's nice.

They both laugh. Carol starts throwing things off the couch on to one of the chairs, one at a time

Lovely place you've got here. (*She pulls a face at Louise*)
Eddie Do you think so?
Carol Oh definitely. I thought I was in t'Ritz for a minute.

They both sit down really close to each other up one end of the settee

> *Eddie comes in with glasses and a corkscrew. He puts them down*

Eddie Here we are.
Carol (*looking behind*) Where's what's-his-name then?
Eddie Oh he's just coming.

The sound of a toilet flush rattling loud, off. Carol and Louise burst out laughing. Eddie just hands out the glasses

> *Brink enters. He goes and sits on an armchair*

Carol Hiyah.

Brink smiles. Louise titters. Eddie is getting the corkscrew in a bottle (He opens two bottles, one red, one white)

Is he t'waiter then?

Brink No, he's just better at it than me.
Carol What a confession.

Louise laughs. Carol stays straight-faced

Brink What? Oh yeah. Ha.

Both girls crack up laughing

Eddie Here we go. (*He gets up to start pouring the wine, to Carol first*)
Carol Hang on, is that white?
Eddie Yeah.
Carol Aw, I wanted red.
Eddie Oh. (*He goes back and gets the red*)
Carol Er no, go on I'll have white.

Eddie changes bottles again

  Oh I don't know though, red's good innit.
Eddie (*laughing*) I'll pour it over your head in a minute.
Carol Oh God Louise, in' he masterful. Go on then pour.

He pours red. He passes on to Louise

  Er waiter, what's your name again?
Eddie Eddie.
Carol Eh, Eddie you know what they say, don't you?
Eddie What?
Carol White and they're up all night. (*She drinks*) Red, they're straight to
  bed.

Louise splutters

Eddie Oh ay, an' who told you that?
Carol (*sipping*) She did.
Louise I never!
Carol Did you not, well I thought you did. Never mind. Carry on. Carry
  on.

He pours some for Brink and himself. They all drink

Brink So what do you do?
Carol What do you fancy?

Louise tuts

Eddie What do you mean?
Carol (*pretending to change the subject*) Er nice wine, in' it?
Louise No.

They both laugh

Eddie (*trying again*) So what do you do?
Brink (*quickly*) To live.

Carol Well I breathe, I can't speak for her like.

Louise splutters

Eddie I don't know, you're quick you two aren't you.
Carol No, you two are slow.

Louise spills her drink on herself, drops the glass. It breaks

Louise Oh look!
Eddie I'll get you a cloth.

Eddie goes off into the kitchen. Brink gets up and goes too

Carol (*shouting*) God, how big is this cloth. Take two corners each then just
   walk in with it.
Louise Oh Carol. Do you not like 'em?
Carol They're OK. But they just think they're great.
Louise Eh? They're a bit of all right though aren't they?
Carol Did you not see 'em at the bar posing off?
Louise I know, but you fancied 'em when you saw 'em.
Carol Maybe I did. Maybe I did. And the way they chatted us up.
Louise I know, but it were good though weren't it? Very different.
Carol You could say that. They just think too much of themselves for my
   liking.
Louise I think they're all right.
Carol Well, no ways are they gettin' the better of me.

*Eddie comes back in. He goes to Louise and gives her a cloth. He gets down
and starts picking up bits of glass*

Carol (*looking round*) Where's he gone again? Is there summat wrong with
   his bowels or what?
Eddie (*laughing*) He's just looking for another glass for Louise.

*Louise gives him back the cloth, he starts mopping up the couch arm and floor
with it*

Brink appears in the doorway

Brink There's not another one. You can have mine.
Louise No, it's all right.
Eddie (*passing it to her*) You're all right, here you are.
Louise Oh I don't want to take your glass. What'll you have?

Carol grabs it out of Eddie's hand

Carol Here get it. Sap. (*She gets the bottle and pours more wine*) Here and
   top it up.
Louise Carol!

*Brink has a mug with him. Eddie sits on the couch with the girls. Brink sits on
the arm of the armchair. Carol looks at Eddie, then looks at Brink*

Carol Eh what's this? Manœuvres. We're being surrounded, Louise cock.
Brink (*to Louise*) Is she always like this?

Louise Yes.
Carol Hang on a minute. Like what?
Brink Like . . .
Carol What!
Brink Aggressive.
Carol In what way? What's that s'pose to mean?
Brink I don't know.
Eddie He's sorry he spoke.
Carol Sorry he spoke. I should think so. I'm not aggressive. (*She grabs Louise, mock-nuts her*) Am I not, Louise love?
Louise (*laughing*) I'm saying nowt.
Carol Anyway, what does mean, aggressive? I'm just having a bit of fun. If you can't take that there's summat wrong with you.
Brink We can take it.
Carol I s'pose you're not used to this, you're used to women just fallin' all over you, aren't you?
Brink Not really, no.
Carol Just fallin' all under you then.

Brink smiles

   Dick.
Brink She's mad.
Eddie She's not.
Carol I am.
Louise She is.

They all laugh. Pause

Eddie (*holding up a bottle high*) Anybody want some more?
Carol (*holding her glass high*) Not yet.

Pause

   How long you lived here?

Brink shrugs

   Well it's certainly a . . . certainly a . . . what's the word I'm looking for?
Eddie Tip?
Carol No, slag heap.

Louise laughs

   That's it . . .
Eddie Eh, well feel free, girls, to put it in order.
Carol You must be a joke.
Louise You must be joking. You want to see the state of her room at home.
Carol Louise shut up givin' away my personals. You'll be tellin' 'em what colour knickers I've got on next. (*She looks at them*) Go on, say it. "If you had any on" or "See-through".
Brink I'm saying nothing.
Carol Oh what gentlemen, or are you just pouffs?

Louise Carol, you're terrible.

Carol Eh, eh Louise don't desert the ranks now. Especially when they're just coming on so strong, eh lads?

They just smile

So now we're round to it. When are you going to move in then, lads. When should we expect the first move?

Brink leans right over and starts kissing her

Get off.

He stops and stands

Get off.

Brink goes back to the chair, unaffected

Brink (*hands up*) I'm off.

She's a bit stunned

Carol (*to compose herself*) I thought I could smell summat.

No-one laughs. Brink sits away in the chair. Eddie drinks

Louise It's nice this place really.

Eddie Really?

Louise (*laughing*) I mean underneath it all. If it was tidied up.

Eddie I s'pose it's not bad it's——

Carol (*to Brink*) So are you not speaking now? (*Not giving him time to answer; to Eddie*) Is he sulking now?

Brink No. Not at all. Nothing like that.

Carol (*looking at them both one to another*) I don't know where I am with you two.

Eddie What do you mean?

Louise (*excited*) You're right different.

Eddie Than what?

Carol (*quick*) Watch it Louise they'll get all big-headed. Well bigger-headed. (*She scrutinizes them both*) What is it with you two?

Brink reaches out and takes Louise's hand. He leads her over towards him, stands and kisses her

Carol looks. She gets up, goes into the kitchen

(*Off*) Is it through here?

Eddie What?

No reply. Eddie realizes she means the toilet

Oh yeah. Yeah. Straight through.

Louise separates from Brink though still in his arms

Brink What is it?

Louise Carol.

Brink looks at her

She's gone off 'cause she likes you really.
Brink (*recognizing something in her*) And what about you, who do you like?

She looks down, a bit embarrassed

You like Eddie really, don't you?

She looks a bit more embarrassed

It's all right. Eddie.

Eddie stands up and takes Louise back with him on to his knee in one single movement

Brink goes off through to the kitchen

Eddie kisses Louise very gently, and again. She puts her hand in his hair. From the kitchen is heard:

Carol (*off*) What's this? Hey. You soon change your tune.

Then movement as Brink kisses her. They enter. He turns the light off

The stage is in darkness. Black. Sounds of kissing and movement. Shuffling. Carols says "No." Movement. Carol says "Get off". Shuffling. Carol turns the light on

That's enough of that.

Carol is standing at the light switch. Louise has moved away from Eddie

What do you think we are?

Brink shrugs

What do you think we are, slags?
Eddie Nooo.
Brink Why did you come back?
Carol Just for something to do.
Brink What about all the lead ons, lead ins?
Louise Don't he talk funny. You were like that in the pub. Lead on, lead ins.
Eddie (*changing the subject*) Anyway.
Louise (*turning on him realizing she should be mad*) Anyway what?
Eddie Eh eh. Don't be bad-tempered. Anyway, more drinks? (*He lifts the bottle*)
Carol You can't get us drunk then start again you know.
Brink Forget it.
Carol Listen to him now. Typical. They're all the same. Can't get their end away they don't wanna know. Do get their end away they don't wanna know.

Eddie Oh come on.

Carol No. I want somethin' else to happen for a change. It's the same every time. Every time some smart-arse spends time and money on you with one thing only in mind. Then upsets you. It's boring and upsetting. I'm sick of it. You think you're just wanted for use. You two seemed a bit interesting, a bit unusual like. I thought I might find something else here. But not so. You're always wrong, aren't you? Nowt's never the way you wanted. You always have to make do. Every single thing's a disappointment.

Louise Carol.

Carol stops

Carol Come on then Louise. (*She gets her bag*)

Louise gets hers; they start leaving

Eddie Come on, have another.

They go for the door. Brink suddenly jumps up really quick, the fastest thing he's done all night, and stands in front of the door

Brink Stay and I promise you something different. Let's see how much difference you can take.

Carol stops in her tracks. So does Louise

You want something different. Stay, I mean it. (*He guides them back to the settee.*) You know what we do for it. To really get a change. We have a something that we always do when outside gets to you. Eddie, shall we show them?

Eddie looks

Come on let's show them. Let's have it out of them.

The girls sit, mystified

Do you like good music?

Carol Yeah. Like what?

Brink Like soul. Real down there soul.

Carol Don't know what you mean.

While he's talking, Eddie is pouring wine in the glasses

Brink What about you, Louise?

Louise Well I like "*Hot Chocolate*".

Brink shakes his head. Eddie is passing around glasses

Eddie Drink.

They hesitate

Brink Drink. Don't worry, go on.

Eddie Go.

They do

Fast though. Fast!

They do

Brink Good.

Eddie is quickly filling up the glasses again

Carol Eh, hang on.

Brink grabs one and drinks it

Eddie Do. Another?
Brink Another.
Carol What are you doing?

The lads are laughing. Eddie fills up again

Brink It's all part of it, you'll see after.
Eddie (*lifting his glass*) Brink old drink.

They cheer and clink glasses, then drink. Louise laughs. Carol does a bit

Brink Come on Eddie, steady.

They lift the glasses and down them. Eddie lets himself fall back. Carol suddenly laughs too

Come on in. Join us.

He touches her chin. She knocks his hand away

Carol All right, set 'em up.
Louise Carol.
Carol Oh what the hell.

Eddie has already set them up. They get a glass each

Brink Down.

He opens his mouth wide first. Eddie too. They down it in one. Carol and Louise laugh and giggle, try it but can't get it down so fast, but manage to shift it. Eddie is opening another two bottles

Carol What about some music then?
Brink Some will be coming soon and ...
Carol And what?
Brink Wait for it, love.
Louise Oooooh.

They drink again

Carol Come on put summat on now, what you got? Let's see.

Eddie drinking, points to the single on the wall

Eh just that one!
Eddie Ay that's it.
Brink One more drink and then it's on.

Eddie Up up.

The glasses are raised

Carol This is mad.
Louise (*laughing*) It is innit.

They drink them down

Carol Music!
Brink Put it on.
Louise Put it on.

Eddie gets up and puts the record on the deck

Carol Bloody hell, I hope I like it.

Brink slowly puts a finger to his mouth to quiet her. Silence. In the silence begins the slow crackling you always get with old records. The record begins. It is "Try a Little Tenderness" by Otis Redding. The volume is up very loud. The record ends. Eddie takes off from there

Eddie Bzzzzzzzzzzzzzzzzzzzz. Raaaaaaaaaaaaaaaaa. Blast off! Wyatt Earp, Wild Bill Hicock, Jesse James, Buffalo Bill, Billy the Kid, Maverick, Jim Bowie, Geronimo, Butch Cassidy, Davy Crockett, Doc Holiday. Eddie, Eddie, Eddie the hero. This is it, you let owt out, show what's below, let go, throw, glow, burn your Giro. I got me suit I got me image, suit, image, (*He sings*) "Who could ask for anything more?" Me! England's in pieces. England's an old twat in the sea. England's cruel. My town's scuffed out. My people's pale. Pale face. (*He pulls a pretend gun*) Bang bang bang. It's a shoot-out with the sheriff. EDDIE, EDDIE, EDDIE, the hero. Don't weaken, or you're Dole and Done, Dole and Done, never weaken, show yoursel' sharp, so sharp you cut. Head up. Eyes hard. Walk like Robert Mitchum. (*He draws and shoots*) Bang, bang, bang, bang, bang, bang, bang. I'm going to lie out now and burn for all I'm worth. (*He stops, lies down*)

Silence. The girl's faces are wide open, stunned and drunk

Brink That's what you do, you drink, you listen to Otis, you get to the bottom of things and let rip.
Louise (*in wonder*) What for?
Brink To stop going mad.
Louise Oh.

Carol is quiet, swigging from the bottle. Hiccups

(*Drunk*) Give us a swig on that.
Carol Does he have to shout?
Brink I'm full of something nasty tonight. A smelly memory I can't wipe off. I'm s'pose to be the strong silent type me but I'm not. It's just a

casing, in casing I get it again. Once I fucked an older woman, hated and fucked her hard on the kitchen floor, knees hitting the fridge, dog bowl in her hair, handfuls of old white skin in my mit. After she'd gone I sat on the lino and cried. My first 'skrike since "No mummy left". I always keep tight in front of people me, I don't want them in, they stink. HANDS OFF FOREVER! I want to be free. I want to be a cowboy, those dream fellows who died for us. Guns and smoke, one more dead, a mouthful of saloon dust. I want cowboy but I'm just cattle, herded, helpless, waiting, aching to be killed, at the mercy of my CUNT-TRAY. Oh God, on I crow. Down I go. I lie to myself. I lie to the Pope. I lie on the rug. I lie with my bedtime cheese. I must stop now because I'm crying real tears, but inside. A man cry. I cry through the dole, hole, times in which we live. Them slag's hands I still feel and I don't know why.

Carol stands

Carol Can I say anything? Can I? I'll say this then. BIG BUST. BIG BUST ON ME BODY. BIG BRA BURSTING BUST. MEN LOOK. How's that? CRACK CRACK CRACK the whip on 'em. Crackoh crack, cut men for their sins. POVERTY. Poverty wants me. He's in my hair and clothes. He comes dust on me knickers. I can't scrape him off. Everythin's soiled you know, our house, me mum, the bath. I'm sick. Nowt's nice around me. Nowt's nice. NOWT'S NICE. Where's finery? Fucked off! Where's soft? Gone hard! I want a walk on the mild side. I want to be clean. Cleaned. Spray me wi' somethin' sweet, spray me away. (*Stated*) Carol has nowt.

Carol sits, falls over to one side, curls up on the couch

Louise It's all gambling this, int it? Gambling with gabble to see what come out. That record, it's so about pure things it make you want to cry. Why's the world so tough? It's like walking through meat in high heels. Nothing's shared out right, money or love. I'm a quiet person me. People think I'm deaf and dumb. I want to say things but it hard. I have big wishes, you know. I want my life to be all shine'id. It's so dull. Everything's so dulled. When that man sings on that record there, you put the flags up. Because he reminds you of them feelings you keep forgetting. The important ones. Once you wrap 'em up and put 'em away, there's nothing left but profit and loss and who shot who? But it's so hard, life. So hard. Nothing's interesting. Everything's been made ordinary in our eyes. I want magic and miracles, I want a Jesus to come and change things again and show the invisible. And not let us keep forgetting, forge-netting everything, kickin' everyone. I want the surface up and off and all the gold and jewels and light out on the pavements. Anyway I never spoke such speech in my life and I'm glad I have. If I keep shouting somehow a somehow I might escape

Eddie Somehow a somehow, might escape.

Pause

Somehow a somehow, might escape.

Brink Somehow a somehow, might escape.

Eddie ⎫
Brink ⎭ (*together*) Somehow a somehow, might escape.

Louise Somehow a somehow, might escape.

Eddie ⎫ (*together*) Somehow a somehow, might escape.
Brink ⎭

Louise

Carol (*coming up*) Somehow.

Eddie ⎫
Carol ⎪
Brink ⎬ (*together*) Somehow a somehow a somehow, might escape.
Louise ⎭

They all move in together

All Somehow a somehow a somehow—(*snatched*)—might escape!

All pressed together, arms and legs round each other

Somehow a somehow a somehow—might escape!

Out to the audience. A chant now

Somehow a somehow a somehow—might escape!
Somehow a somehow a somehow—might escape!
Somehow a somehow a somehow—might escape!

Faster

Somehow a somehow a somehow—might escape!
Somehow a somehow a somehow—might escape!
Somehow a somehow a somehow—might escape!

Very fast and loud

SOMEHOW A SOMEHOW A SOMEHOW—MIGHT ESCAPE!
SOMEHOW A SOMEHOW A SOMEHOW—MIGHT ESCAPE!
SOMEHOW A SOMEHOW A SOMEHOW—MIGHT ESCAPE!

Loud and massive

SOMEHOOOOOOOOOOOOOOOOOO——

Black-out

—OOOOOOOOOOOOOOOOOW

Silence

The Lights come up on the Road

Scullery is just sliding his back down the wall to sit

Scullery Well it coming up to morning nar. I'll ha' a last fag and a last sup then I'll go whome. (*He takes a fag packet out, opens it; it's empty. He takes a bottle out of his pocket, puts it to his mouth; nothing in it. He turns it upside down; empty. He lets his head flop forward*)

The Lights dim on him. The sound of shoes dropping in the dark. The Lights come up on Helen in her room. She is sitting taking her shoes off. She strolls over to the bed, sits on it, lies down. The Lights dim. The sound of dreamy humming. The Lights come up on Jerry darning his sock, humming a good old tune. The Lights dim. The sound of a bottle rolling. The Lights come up on the four in Brink's room. Brink is asleep on the couch, Carol is asleep on the floor, her hand gently rolling a bottle. Eddie and Louise are standing in the centre of the room locked in an embrace, slowly swaying to some imagined music. The Lights dim, then come up on Scullery, who is preparing to sleep where he is

If you're ever in the area call again. (*He lies down*) Call again.

Black-out

PRODUCTION NOTES

Page 8

In the Royal Court production Eddie had his own cassette player and an unspoken battle ensued; as one turned his volume up the other turned his higher etc

There is a shorter version of **Act I** which may be preferred, viz:

As written until Eddie and Dad scene. Follow with Molly scene, then to Scullery, Eddie and Brink cross: Lane and Dor: and Skinlad's cross, section. Then to Skinlad's speech, then to Scullery and derelict house (cut Brenda and Scullery). Then to Jerry's speech. Then to Scullery, Blowpipe and Molly scene (cut Clare's cross). Then to Joey and Clare. Then as written

Page 17

In the Royal Court production, the Balds were played by one actor doing two voices

Page 26

A shorter version of this scene is as follows:

It should appear that he's going to get out of bed to really kill somebody. Then Clare wakes. She puts her arm on him

Clare Joey.

Joey Eh?

Clare Joey, I feel so faint and white. I can hardly see my Joey.

Joey Don't worry about it. There might be a message or a sign soon. You never can tell when it's a going to come on you. Fuck me I wish I could sweat or something, I'm like paper.

Silence

Clare Joe, is my skin cracking?

Joey No.

Clare Around my mouth at the corners is there any cracking?

Joey (*after a quick glance*) No.

Clare It feels like it is. (*She starts to sing to herself, very softly*) "Don't know much about history. Don't know much about society. But I do know that I love you and I know if you'd love me too what a wonderful world this would be. What a wonderful world this would be."

Silence

I love you so much, Joey.

Joey Eh?

Clare I love you, my man. Perhaps if I cried you could drink up my tears.

Joey Be quiet now.

Clare Joey is it death-time?

Joey (*shocked*) Stop it! You're talking now like you've never talked in your
life.
Clare Where's it coming from?
Joey Oh no. You're more advanced now than me. You're going some-
where. A state. Into a state.
Clare Eh?
Joey Just shout out things. That's how I'll test you. Just say things what
come into your head.
Clare I'm so knackered out. A feel I'm just holding on by the threads. One
or two fine wet threads, the rest have dried an' broke.
Joey Oh my dear.
Clare Don't worry. I still love you, that's left. I keep on seeing faces, like me
dad's, me mum's, me dad's again. I still want to cry when I see me dad's
dismantled face. He lost his last job you know. Just think one day there
might be the last job on earth. And everyone will come out to see the man
lose it. They'll all watch as he comes up to his last hour. The last hooter
blow whoooooooooooo oh ooooooo oooooooooooo oooooo I'm being corny
now, int a Joey? Oh my it's white in here behind the eyes, so misty. (*She
closes her eyes*)

Joey holds her. He makes a fist

Page 42
If the theatre is not big enough to take the run around of the long row, then
this shorter version can be used

A rattling is heard getting louder and louder

> *Suddenly Scullery enters pushing a shopping trolley at mad speed across the
> stage*

Scullery Ayeeeeeeeeeeeeeeeeeeeeee! (*He turns it and comes back to centre*)
Ayeeeeeeeeeeeeeeeeeeeeeee!

> *As this happens Brian comes on pursued by Marion*

Marion Come here you!
Brian Aw piss off!
Marion What's the fucking big idea?!
Brian Aw fuck off, woman!
Marion I'll fuck nowhere. You stand still!

Scullery is enjoying this. He sits in the trolley to watch

Brian Go with your little friend.
Marion Oh you nasty-minded bugger!

*She grabs him, makes him stop. They end up on each side of the trolley,
Scullery smack in the middle*

You're a selfish bastard you, Brian. Me myself an' I! Me myself an' I.
Brian Aw fuck off.
Marion You know what your pissing problem is don't you eh?

Brian What?
Marion You don't know how to treat a woman.
Brian You know what your pissin' problem is don't you?
Marion What!
Brian You're not woman, you're tart.

She loses her temper more, goes for him, but he spins the trolley round between them. Now they're on opposite sides from before

Marion FART!
Brian TART!

Madder still at this, she gives chase again. Again he spins round putting the trolley between them

Marion (*unable to get at him*) Arrrrrrgh!

Brink and Eddie, Carol and Louise enter. They see the row and watch

I'll kill you Brian! I'll kill! I'm not joking!

Brian laughs and exits

Brink Go on, love!
Marion Piss off! OR YOU'LL PISSIN' GET IT!
Brink Promises.

She hits at Brink with her handbag. They are all laughing

Marion Eh eh come back you! I've not finished wi' you!

Carol and Louise pass Scullery

Scullery Hey I'm on special offer; don't miss your bargain, girls.

Carol and Louise look at each other, smile, grab the trolley and shove him off

OOOhhhhhhhhhhhhhhhhhhhhhhhhhhhhhhhhhhhh.

FURNITURE AND PROPERTY LIST

PRE-SHOW

In theatre bar:
        Dartboard, darts, blackboard, chalk
        Tiny stage with mike and glitter curtain
        Posters etc.

Personal: **Barry:** cigarettes, lighter

ACT I

The Road:
On stage: Broken road sign (remains onstage throughout)

Louise's living-room:
On stage: Chair
        Oily engine on spread-out newspapers
        Mirror on wall

Off stage: Hairbrush **(Louise)**

Personal: **Brother:** dirty hands, £2 in pocket

Brenda's living room:
On stage: Armchair
        Ironing-board. *On it:* iron, dress
        Carol's coat. *In pocket:* loose change

Personal: **Brenda:** lighted cigarette

The Road:
Off stage Bottle of drink **(Scullery)**

Personal: **Brink:** cigarettes, lighter

Eddie's living-room
On stage: Armchair. *By it:* Hoover (practical), tools TV
        Mirror on wall
        Table. *On it:* pan, ashtray
        Chair. *On it:* shirt, anti-perspirant, tie, aftershave, jacket
        Comb for **Eddie**

The Road:
Personal: **Scullery:** bottle

Molly's room:
On stage: Sink and taps (practical). *In it:* bucket. *Under it:* saucer of milk
        Table. *On it:* box of old make-up, mirror, cup, teabags, hairbrush
        Chair
        Gas cooker (practical). *On it:* kettle, matches

The Road:
Off stage: Long cardboard box tied with string, containing papers, battered portable
cassette recorder with mike **(Professor)**
2 cigarettes **(Chantal)**
Piece of paper **(Stage Management)**

Personal: **Scullery:** lighter

Skin-Lad's room:
On stage: Wooden chair
Bare light bulb dangling

The Road:
On stage: Window with sacking over it
Drainpipe or scaffolding up to window
Behind window: doll, burnt newspaper, Christmas card, old tap, basket,
crucifix, musical box

Personal: **Scullery:** pillow-case in pocket

Jerry's room:
On stage: Armchair. *By it:* shoes, polish, brush, tie
Ironing-board, iron

The Road:
On stage: Dustbin and lid

Off stage Empty beer crate, bottle of drink **(Blowpipe)**
Bed and bedding **(Scullery)**

Joey's room:
On stage: Bed and bedding

Off stage: Pack of leaflets **(Bisto)**

The Road:
Off stage: Cassette recorder with mike **(Professor)**

Personal: **Scullery:** comb and mirror

Joey's room:
On stage: Bed and bedding

INTERVAL

On stage: Disco equipment

ACT II

Personal: **Scullery:** music box (practical)

Chip shop:
On stage: Counter. *Behind it:* chips, bags, etc.

Personal: **Dor, Lane:** money

Off stage: Bags of chips **(Dor** and **Lane)**

The Road:
On stage: Lamp-post

Off stage: Bag of chips **(Scullery)**
             Bag of chips **(Curt)**

Helen's room:
On stage: Armchair
            Bed
            Pouffe
            TV
            Record player
            Records without sleeves on floor, some in wire rack
            Sideboard

Off stage: 2 plates, one with chips, pudding, peas, one with fish, chips, hair **(Helen)**
             Dirty old towel, flannel **(Helen)**
             Piece of toilet roll **(Helen)**

Personal: **Soldier:** "vomit" in mouth

The Road:
On stage: Bench

Off stage: Bag with chip in it **(Scullery)**
             Pool cue **(Barry)**
             Opener thrown on **(Bald)**
             Tankard **(Bald)**

Personal: **Dor:** matches
            Barry: cigarettes, 2 bottles of beer in pockets

Valerie's room:
On stage: Hard kitchen chair

Personal: **Valerie:** lighted cigarette

Chantal:
Personal: **Chantal:** cigarette

The Road:
Personal: **Blowpipe:** bottle of rum in pocket

Brian's living-room:
On stage: Couch
            Sideboard. *In it:* bottles of sherry
            Record player, records

Off stage: Blood on thumb **(Marion)**
             Pint glass **(Barry)**

Personal: **Marion:** handbag containing paper tissues

The Road:
Off stage: Shopping trolley **(Scullery)**

Personal: **Marion:** handbag

Brink's place:
On stage: Long settee. *On it:* clothes, clutter, etc.
            2 chairs
            Massive stereo speaker
            Flat record deck
            On wall: single record on gold nail

Off stage: 5 bottles of wine (red and white) **(Eddie)**
              4 glasses, corkscrew **(Eddie)**
              Cloth **(Eddie)**
              Mug **(Brink)**

Personal: **Carol, Louise:** handbags

The Road:
On stage: Wall

Personal: **Scullery:** empty cigarette packet, empty bottle in pocket

Helen's room, Jerry's room, Brink's room:
On stage: As before

Personal: **Jerry:** sock and darning needle and thread

LIGHTING PLOT

Practical fittings required: TV light effect, pendant in Skin-Lad's room

ACT I

To open: Blackness

Cue 1	As Scullery's match goes out *Spot up on Scullery's face*	(Page 3)
Cue 2	**Scullery** laughs uproariously *Black-out, then lights up on Louise's living-room*	(Page 4)
Cue 3	**Brother:** "... long life innit." *Black-out, then lights up on Brenda's living room*	(Page 5)
Cue 4	**Brenda:** "... long life innit." *Black-out, then lights up on Road*	(Page 7)
Cue 5	**Scullery:** "Let's have a see" *Black-out, then lights up on Eddie's living-room; TV effect on*	(Page 8)
Cue 6	**Eddie's Dad** turns off TV *Cut TV effect*	(Page 9)
Cue 7	After **Eddie's Dad** has vacuumed for a few moments *Black-out, then lights up on **Scullery** and Road*	(Page 9)
Cue 8	**Lane:** "Start wi' France." They kiss *Black-out*	(Page 11)
Cue 9	Sound of someone crying stops. Silence *Lights up on Molly's room*	(Page 11)
Cue 10	**Molly** picks up the little mirror and carries on *Black-out, then lights up on **Professor** and Road*	(Page 12)
Cue 11	**Scullery** drops screwed-up paper down his pants *Black-out, then lights up on **Skin-Lad**—bare light bulb dangling*	(Page 14)
Cue 12	**Skin-Lad:** "... with the dharma. Om." *Black-out, then lights up on Road*	(Page 15)
Cue 13	**Scullery** looks out at audience in disbelief *Black-out, then lights up on Jerry's room*	(Page 17)
Cue 14	**Jerry:** "... me, us, them or God." *Black-out, then lights up on Road*	(Page 18)
Cue 15	**Molly** finishes song *Dim lights*	(Page 19)

Cue 16	**Scullery** pushes bed c *Bring up spot on bed*	(Page 19)
Cue 17	**Scullery** goes off *Black-out*	(Page 20)
Cue 18	**Mother's voice:** "JOEY!!" Silence *Bring up lights on Joey's room*	(Page 20)
Cue 19	**Clare** gets into bed with **Joey** *Black-out, then either: lights up on* **Bisto** *(if his speech is used),* *cross-fading to lights on Joey's room after* **Bisto** *exits; or:* *pause, then lights up on Joey's room*	(Page 21)
Cue 20	Loud knocking starts on door (Joey kisses Clare) *Black-out, the lights up on Road*	(Page 25)
Cue 21	**Scullery** laughs uproariously as he exits on **Professor's** *back* *Black-out, then lights up on Joey's room*	(Page 25)
Cue 22	**Joey** puts his hand in front of his face and bites into it *Black-out, then lights up on Joey's room*	(Page 28)
Cue 23	**Scullery:** "See you soon." *Fade to black-out*	(Page 28)

INTERVAL

Bring up lights a little, pause to establish interval, then snap up disco lighting

ACT II

To open: Spot on **Scullery**

Cue 24	**Scullery** exits *Cross-fade to chip shop*	(Page 31)
Cue 25	**Manfred:** "... COME AND BUY ..." *Cross-fade to* **Dor** *and* **Lane** *up eating chips*	(Page 32)
Cue 26	**Lane:** "Come on." *Cross-fade to Road*	(Page 32)
Cue 27	**Curt** goes off *Black-out, then spot on armchair* c; *after a few moments increase* *lighting on Helen's room*	(Page 33)
Cue 28	**Helen** closes her eyes and puts her head back *Black-out, then lights up on Road—blue light and spinning lights* *from silver ball*	(Page 35)
Cue 29	**Scullery** throws chip paper at **Jerry** *Cut blue and spinning lights; black-out as* **Jerry** *strolls off, then* *lights up on Road*	(Page 35)
Cue 30	**Mrs Bald** (*off*): "He he he." *Black-out, then lights up on Valerie's room*	(Page 37)

Cue 31	**Valerie:** "Can we not?" *Black-out, then lights up on* **Chantal**	(Page 38)
Cue 32	**Bald** disappears *Black-out, then lights up on Road*	(Page 38)
Cue 33	**Marion** and **Brian** go off on the other side from **Scullery** *Cross-fade to living-room*	(Page 39)
Cue 34	**Linda** (*to audience, mocking*) : "POOR LITTLE ME!" *Cross-fade to Road*	(Page 42)
Cue 35	**Marion** and **Brian** appear at the very top gallery *Spotlights on them*	(Page 44)
Cue 36	**Marion:** "... BLEEDING FUCK!" *Black-out, then lights up on Brink's place—living-room and kitchen area, off*	(Page 44)
Cue 37	**Carol** (*off*): "... soon change your tune." Movement *Snap off light in kitchen area*	(Page 50)
Cue 38	**Brink** turns off light in living-room *Black-out*	(Page 50)
Cue 39	**Carol:** "Get off." Shuffling. **Carol** turns light on *Snap up light in living-room*	(Page 50)
Cue 40	**All:** "SOMEHOOOOOOOOOOOO——" *Black-out, then lights up on Road*	(Page 55)
Cue 41	**Scullery** lets his head flop forwards *Dim lights on* **Scullery**, *pause then bring up lights on Helen's room*	(Page 56)
Cue 42	**Helen** sits on bed, lies down *Dim lights on Helen's room, pause, then lights on Jerry's room; dim lights on Jerry's room; pause, then lights up on Brink's room; after a few moments, cross-fade to* **Scullery**	(Page 56)
Cue 43	**Scullery:** "Call again." *Black-out*	(Page 56)

EFFECTS PLOT

ACT I

Cue 1   Before the play begins   (Page 3)
          "Somewhere Over the Rainbow" by Judy Garland plays

Cue 2   As lights come up on Eddie's living-room   (Page 8)
          Bring up TV sound effect, full blast

Cue 3   **Eddie** puts on aftershave   (Page 9)
          Loud knocking on wall

Cue 4   **Eddie's Dad** turns off TV, plugs in Hoover   (Page 9)
          Cut TV sound; bring up Hoover noise—cut after a few moments

Cue 5   Black-out. Silence   (Page 11)
          Sound of window opening; voice at breaking point: "Fucking
          *   fuck"; window closes; silence; dog starts barking, then stops;*
          *   sound of someone crying; silence*

Cue 6   **Scullery** draws on fag   (Page 14)
          Sound of window opening, "Dynasty" theme tune on TV inside;
          *   window closes*

Cue 7   Black-out   (Page 18)
          Sound of dustbin lid falling down

Cue 8   **Scullery: "JOEY'S STORY."** Darkness   (Page 19)
          Loud knocking starts, then stops

Cue 9   **Joey:** "... I'm knacked."   (Page 20)
          Loud knock on door

Cue 10 **Clare:** "... let me go in."   (Page 20)
          Door is unlocked

Cue 11 **Mother's voice** (*off*): "Oh Clare. Oh."   (Page 22)
          Sound of her going down steps, off

Cue 12 **Clare** screams   (Page 25)
          Loud knocking starts on door—fade after a few moments

INTERVAL

DJ Bisto plays records as per script

ACT II

Cue 13 **Helen** puts on record   (Page 34)
          Music: Barry Manilow or Frank Sinatra

| *Cue* 14 | **Helen** changes record | (Page 34) |
| | *Music: James Brown "Sex Machine"— increase volume as she turns it up* | |

| *Cue* 15 | **Soldier** slides off her into record player | (Page 35) |
| | *Cut music* | |

| *Cue* 16 | Back to the Road. Blue light, spinning lights | (Page 35) |
| | *Music: Engelbert Humperdinck "The Last Waltz"* | |

| *Cue* 17 | **Scullery** throws chip paper at **Jerry** | (Page 35) |
| | *Cut music* | |

| *Cue* 18 | **Brian** puts record on | (Page 40) |
| | *Country and Western music, very loud* | |

| *Cue* 19 | **Brian** turns music down | (Page 41) |
| | *Lower volume of music* | |

| *Cue* 20 | **Marion** gets up and goes out the door | (Page 41) |
| | *Pause, then front door slams, off* | |

| *Cue* 21 | **Linda** (*to audience, mocking*): "POOR LITTLE ME!" | (Page 42) |
| | *Fade music* | |

| *Cue* 22 | **Eddie:** "Oh he's just coming." | (Page 45) |
| | *Toilet flushes loudly, off* | |

| *Cue* 23 | **Eddie** puts record on deck | (Page 53) |
| | *Silence, then slow crackling, then music: "Try a Little Tenderness" by Otis Redding, very loud* | |

| *Cue* 24 | **Brink** puts on record | (Page 53) |
| | *Repeat Cue 23* | |

MADE AND PRINTED IN GREAT BRITAIN BY
LATIMER TREND & COMPANY LTD PLYMOUTH

MADE IN ENGLAND